ONE STOP
Negotiation

DAVID MARTIN and JOHN WYBORN

ICSA Publishing
The Official Publishing Company of
The Institute of Chartered Secretaries and Administrators

in association with

Prentice Hall

London New York Toronto Sydney Tokyo Singapore
Madrid Mexico City Munich Paris

First published 1997 by
ICSA Publishing Limited
Campus 400, Maylands Avenue
Hemel Hempstead
Hertfordshire, HP2 7EZ

Typeset in 10/12.5 pt Meridien with Frutiger Light
by Hart McLeod, Cambridge

Printed and bound in Great Britain
by MPG Books Ltd, Bodmin, Cornwall

British Library Cataloguing in Publication Data

A catalogue record for this book is available from
the British Library

ISBN: 1–860–72042–0

2 3 4 5 6 02 01 00 99

ONE STOP NEGOTIATION

**This book is to be returned on or before
the last date stamped below.**

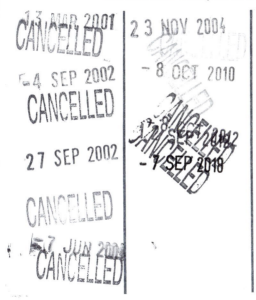

The One Stop Series

Series editor: David Martin, FCIS, FIPD, FCB
Buddenbrook Consultancy

A series of practical, user-friendly yet authoritative titles designed to provide a one stop guide to key topics in business administration.

Other books in the series to date include:

David Martin	*One Stop Company Secretary*
David Martin	*One Stop Personnel*
Jeremy Stranks	*One Stop Health and Safety*
John Wyborn	*One Stop Contracts*

1997 titles:

David Martin	*One Stop Property*
Robert Leach	*One Stop Payroll*
Harris Rosenberg	*One Stop Finance*
Karen Huntingford	*One Stop Insurance*
Robin Ellison	*One Stop Pensions*

Contents

CONTENTS

Preface

Negotiation is not a science nor is it a branch of technology. It is a life skill. We start to negotiate when we are very young indeed: too young, in fact, to realise fully what we are doing. All we learn as infants is that certain kinds of behaviour secure what we want. Other kinds of behaviour do not work at all, and we get punished for it.

As we grow older, we build up patterns of behaviour that reflect what we feel 'works for us'. This will be based partly upon the kind of personality we may have inherited, and partly upon the environment in which we have lived and grown up. The world in which we operate as adults is more complicated, yet the need to understand it is all the greater. This book sets out to approach negotiating from a number of angles.

Part 1 of the book looks at strategy, which can be especially important in building long-term business relationships with other people of a kind whereby *everybody* wins, not just the toughest negotiator.

Part 2 looks at the tactics – how to recognise the 'tricks' that can be played in negotiating, how to play them yourself, how to recognise them when they are played against you, and how to prepare antidotes to those devices that tend to operate against you. Tactics win the battle, but the strategy wins the war.

There is sometimes a perception that negotiating in business is all about facts, costs, profits and logical decision-making. In negotiating, nothing can be further from the truth. Of course it *includes* such matters, but it is also about people, their emotions, their goals, and the kind of human beings they are. An understanding of people's motivation and how their personalities can affect their behaviour can be vital in discovering how best to do business with them.

On the whole, women make better negotiators than men. There are two reasons for this. The first is that their intuitive powers tend to be stronger. The second is that they talk less and listen more. Unfortunately, the English language is not helpful to us. there is no 'common' or 'neutral' gender available. Rather than refer throughout to 'he or she', we have settled in most instances for the traditional 'he' in the text.

In common with the rest of the 'One Stop' series, this book uses the expanded index format. This means that for the most part each subject appears in alphabetical order so that you can find it quickly. Negotiation, however, is not all about ploy and counter-ploy. An important part of it has to do with *understanding* what you are about, *preparing for it*, and *gaining experience*. For this reason, the opening sections consider strategy, psychological factors and preparation. We suggest you read these passages in the order they are presented to help you gain *structure* in your negotiating methods. Then, when you are happy that you can prepare a *plan* for negotiating, turn to the *tactics* in alphabetical order, in order to prepare yourself for the cut and thrust of negotiating 'in the field'.

The more you practise, the better you will become. For this reason we have provided space for notes at the end of each section. Record some of the occasions when you have used the techniques we have described, list what worked and what didn't work. See if you can analyse *why* the various approaches were successful or unsuccessful. Discuss them with friends or colleagues. Do not feel that negotiating is a solo operation. The more you can share experiences with others and obtain second opinions, the better negotiator you will become.

The importance of being prepared for negotiation cannot be over-emphasised. Yet it is often ignored in practice. People imagine that if you are good at negotiating, whatever that means, you will know how to go into a meeting and come out with a better deal than someone who is less good at it. The best negotiators know that, unless they are adequately prepared, they will be at the mercy of forces and influences they have not studied and therefore do not understand. Not all of the techniques we have listed in this book, played to the full, will bring a satisfactory outcome to the person who has not done his or her homework, and who therefore may not recognise a good or a bad deal when he or she sees one. For that reason a section on preparation is presented at the front, as part of the 'core curriculum' that everyone should read and think about first of all.

The other party with whom you are negotiating may not have read any of the books on the subject, may not give a fig for an ongoing relationship, nor for any niceties, and may just be determined to get his own way. It may be difficult to make any progress in this scenario.

There are absolutely NO guarantees in this matter. Whilst on balance the skilled, experienced practitioner will outperform the novice, there have been instances where quite the reverse has been true. The most that effective negotiating will do is to *maximise one's chances* of a successful outcome and *minimise the risks* of failure, however we choose to define it. There will be times when an opportunity is so good that we cannot lose, and other times when the going is so tough that whatever we do will not succeed. However, if we have studied the subject, we shall improve the likelihood of recognising both of these extremes, so that we never lose what is winnable and only concede that which is truly beyond our grasp.

David Martin and John Wyborn
July 1997

PART 1
Strategy

A negotiating strategy

Introduction

It is often argued that strategy in negotiating always works. If this means taking time to plan and prepare before we start, that argument is sound. It is probably more helpful, however, to state that strategy works *best* when there is likely to be a continuing business relationship with the other side, whoever they are. It is in such instances that it is worth taking the time and the trouble to consider what kind of trust can be built up, and working at it.

Preparing to negotiate

First let us ask ourselves what scope for bargaining may exist. In a 'perfect market' such as the Stock Exchange, for instance, there may be little scope. If there are only one or two market-makers, and their prices and dealings are known to all, we may be restricted to negotiating about brokers' rates of commission and little else. We need to decide whether we want advice or merely a dealing-only service. If the volumes of business we have to offer are substantial, this may make us a sufficiently valuable client to justify special rates. If it does, then it may help to know what others have achieved by way of discounts, so that we have a feel for what others may consider a 'good deal'.

Now let us consider another instance: buying a car. Here wider possibilities for negotiation open up. We may be buying a new vehicle. If so, we can study the list prices and try to persuade the dealer to 'knock down' the price for cash. For a hire purchase arrangement, the dealer may get some extra commission, and we can try to bargain for some of this. If there is a used car to trade in, we can negotiate what price we might get for it. We can bargain about the length and extent of the warranty, for extras, such as delivery, insurance, road tax, and so on. Our chosen model may be freely available in any forecourt, or there may be a scarcity so that we might have to wait. This could influence our bargaining power.

Just as the range of possibilities open up, so do the prospects of 'getting it wrong' simply because we may lack practice or do not know the market. We need to consider what is going on, and what we can learn from it.

Identifying needs – and recording them

It is hard to overestimate the value of writing down exactly what we want to achieve before we start. Without a written specification, we might end up buying almost anything – and living to regret it. So what should we write down?

In dealing with motor cars, the first question to ask ourselves is what it is that we really want.

This may be expressed in terms of a single model, brand new or second-hand, or a specification of use. In the latter case, we need to consider the purpose to which it will be put; the number of people who will normally ride in it; the distances they will travel; the annual mileage; whether it has to be suitable for business use, or will be primarily a family car.

By consulting a guide, we might discover that there are a number of models that will fit our requirements. The results of this discovery can be twofold. Firstly, we have begun to learn about the market. Secondly, we have widened our options. Instead of going to negotiate with one main dealer for one model of car, we discover we can talk to half a dozen. This greatly strengthens our bargaining position.

Making time for research

At this point we may decide to get a book of car prices, new and used. If we have contacts in the trade we shall probably take a look at Glass's *Guide*. If not, we may get a copy of one of the high street guides such as Parker's. This will begin to tell us as much as the salesman is likely to know before we have even spoken to him. We shall discover, for instance, that there are differences between prices new, prices at which reputable dealers will sell at second hand, prices that we might expect to obtain buying or selling privately, and prices that might apply at auction sales. We shall also learn that differences in specification might affect the price, and – most of all – the number of miles travelled by the vehicle. When we have done all this, we are in a position to suggest to ourselves the kinds of price range we might expect to deal at, buying new and trading-in or selling second-hand. And knowledge gives us self-confidence and power in negotiating.

Of course, we may well find that the first thing a dealer says when we start talking is '…you can forget all that. We do not use Parker's *Guide* here. I have my own book, laid down by the management…'

This should not worry us unduly. We do not *have* to use Parker's *Guide* ourselves. We have merely chosen to use it, to teach us something about the market-place, and possibly as a benchmark against which to base all of the offers to do business that we may receive. We might, if we wish, compare a series of offers we get in terms of 'so many hundreds of pounds higher, or lower, than our Guide prices'. And according to the urgency of our needs we may decide to accept the highest, the lowest, or indeed none of the offers we get. Meanwhile, we have given ourselves some valuable bargaining counters in the discussions: 'Ah, but you are offering me the 2-litre model, which is less valuable than the 2.5.' 'Over 50,000 miles on the clock. This is above average for the year, and I should expect a £2,000 reduction for that.'

All of that becomes a lot easier when we have done our homework and written it down in some form before the first stages of negotiating even begin. Our list of points to consider now looks like this:

1. Specification of needs
2. Where those needs may be satisfied
3. The various options
4. Room for negotiation
5. Range of prices or costs

It may be worth asking who the parties to a negotiation actually are. Certainly it includes the people who sit round the table doing a deal, but there may be others. How about our spouses or business partners? Perhaps they have additional needs. Let's add them to our written specification.

6. Parties within our own organisation to be considered.
7. Additional needs to be included in the main specification.

Making room for negotiation

The manner in which we negotiate depends in part on whether we are forging a long-term relationship or are considering a 'once-only' deal.

'IF...' and 'THEN...'

Unless we are a company fleet manager, buying a car is likely to be a one-off deal. A common method in such situations is often described as the 'IF... THEN...' approach. Both sides start from their 'at best' positions. Having explored the ground and having established that there is some prospect of ultimate agreement, each cautiously reveals ancillary needs, indicating that 'IF....' the other party were willing to consider satisfying them 'THEN...' we may be prepared to modify the price, or some other factor.

The difficulty with such an approach is that it tends to favour the experienced or 'tough' bargainer, who knows the market best and may start from a higher opening bid. The risk is that ultimately a 'split the difference' deal is struck because one side puts it forward as being 'reasonable' in the circumstances.

A problem can arise if the other party afterwards considers they have been 'fleeced'. They will be untiring in their efforts to squeeze the last drop out of their opponent, regardless of the economics.

Many of us will have experienced this in buying and selling houses. Weeks of house-hunting, followed by days of careful negotiation, have resulted in a bargain involving tens or hundreds of thousands of pounds. A deal is agreed, but the buyer feels the price is pretty steep. The seller, however, reckons the house is going for a song.

Consequently the seller tries – and often fails – to sell a series of minor fixtures such as brass chandeliers at their nearly new prices, and the buyer refuses to buy them. The seller then spends time and considerable inconvenience on the day of the move taking them down. They do not fit his new house, of course, and ultimately end up in a car boot sale.

Meanwhile the first thing the new owner has to do is go out and buy another set of fittings which fit the same screw holes, roundly cursing the vendor for his pettiness. Neither are DIY enthusiasts, but injured feelings have taken over.

Principled negotiating – an alternative to 'IF...' and 'THEN...'

Large-scale or ongoing negotiations demand a different approach. Probably the best book on the techniques developed for such negotiations is *Getting to Yes*, written by Fisher and Ury, members of the Harvard Law School negotiating project in the 1970s (published by Hutchinson, 1981). The Harvard approach seeks to avoid the adversarial approach of 'I want', and is centred upon the premise that it pays to argue for a settlement based upon the *merits of the case*; that people can bargain more persuasively and convincingly for causes in which they can believe; and that settlements based upon what can be demonstrated as 'fair' against some objective criteria stand much more chance of success than those that are based upon 'win' or 'lose' in the bargaining, or which are 'split down the middle' compromises merely to obtain some kind of result. The Harvard Law School calls its approach 'principled negotiation'.

Let us consider the key factors that make 'principled negotiating' work.

Avoiding fixed positions

The first step is to avoid taking up fixed positions – upon anything. The car salesman may have a fixed price for his new car. The more we attack it as 'extortionate' the more he will defend it, until neither of us can shift our positions without losing face. Let no one say that 'face' does not matter. Not only do we have to tell *ourselves* that the deal was a sound one, but the salesman has to sell it to his boss, and we to our partner or our boss. Where a number of organisations or departments are concerned, fixed positions become even more difficult in negotiating.

Before commenting or taking any fixed positions on opening demands, we must take a look at the interests of each party. We need a new car to carry out a number of tasks. It is in our interest that the car should be in good condition, that the mileage rate and fuel consumption should be acceptable, that there should be a warranty for a prudent period, and that the car should be a model that will not depreciate too quickly. We must be prepared to pay a *fair and reasonable* price, bearing in mind the state of the market, how popular the model is, how much the dealer could get for it elsewhere, and so on. There may be other factors on the dealer's side, like the desirability of doing a deal by the end of the quarter when his commission period ends, which he may or may not be willing to discuss.

The Harvard Law School objection is that each side tends to take fixed positions from which later somebody has to move. Typically the seller starts with a high price. The buyer starts with a low offer. The 'canny' or tough negotiator will concede very slowly and by small amounts. Each concession may be made conditional upon reciprocal concessions from the other side. Neither party will wish to reveal more than they have to about their own situation, in case such knowledge is exploited by the other side. If there are common interests, they tend to be discovered more by accident than by design, and in some cases may be regarded as peripheral to the main negotiating processes.

Where each concession represents a 'giving way' from the initial position struck, a good deal of 'saving face' may have to be done. Indeed such negotiations, and their outcomes, are often made subject to 'no publication' provisions to ensure that only those directly associated with the deal are subsequently aware of all that went on. One is sometimes reminded of the cartoon conversation between the boss and his subordinate:

Boss: 'Harris, I have to make it quite clear that your new salary is strictly confidential, and is not to be discussed with anyone. Do I make that clear?'

Harris: 'Perfectly, sir. There is no problem. I am as ashamed of it as you are.'

Whether such reflections are spoken or merely felt by each participant, they do represent much that is negative at the end of adversarial negotiations.

The 'IF... THEN...' and the 'splitting the difference' that often concludes such a contest can leave each party feeling the other has got a better deal than they deserved. No one has considered the positive aspects, because in the battleground those aspects tend to represent 'no man's land'. Little thought has been given to long-term relationships. It is assumed that sellers will always try to get the highest prices for the least cost, and thus that buyers have to be tough, unyielding people who will always seek competitive bids whenever they can, each time playing off one against the other, and demonstrating 'muscle' wherever possible.

This battery of assumptions can be difficult enough with two parties. Where there are many participants to a deal, however, it can become almost impossible. Someone has to become 'soft' against the other 'hard' positions to reach agreement at all. That party will be all too aware that they have given way to pressure, and they may be untiring in their efforts to 'get back' at the others later in the relationship. It helps to foster a climate where everybody accepts an initial loss on each contract, knowing full well that they are going to find ways of making their profits from the variation orders and extension business, most of which will not go through normal negotiating channels.

Therefore, the greater the number of alternative approaches that are discussed, the further one gets from fixed positions and the greater the opportunity for a solution that suits everyone. By insisting that separate and objective criteria are used (to decide what is 'fair and reasonable', for instance) one gets away from the people, their personal egos and positions.

Seeking to solve problems

When 'principled negotiators' operate, they are seeking to *solve problems*, to deal wisely, to focus on the *principles*, so that personal trust becomes less of an issue. They will not fix an 'at best' or 'at worst' position, at least not at the outset, and they will parry the 'hard' or 'tough' demand: 'I accept that you are insisting on this, but let us consider whether it is a *reasonable* position to take.' Wherever possible, they will seek external measures, not personal opinions, of what is 'reasonable'.

Whilst taking human factors fully into account, they will concentrate upon the problems and the opportunities of solving them rather than upon human reactions that have to do with the mere process of negotiation. They will not solve human problems by making concessions.

The Harvard approach hinges upon many points. One of these is the *separation of the people from the problem.*

Separating the people from the problem

People in business need to achieve, and to be seen to be achieving, organisational goals: 'the best price', 'the highest quality', 'delivery on time', 'no items out of stock' and so on. They also need to form relationships with the people with whom they deal (some more than others, according to their personality). Confrontational bargaining always puts these needs in conflict with one another.

It is always worthwhile for a negotiator to take time to analyse the other person's viewpoint as well as his own. Sometimes this will be an inverse attitude to his own. One person views a glass of water half-full, another as half-empty. At other times the view can be more judgmental. 'I always provide support to him whenever I am asked' can also be interpreted as 'He *only* provides support when I *ask* him.'

The difference here is one of perception, not substance. Time taken to perceive the other side can always be of value.

We need to consider a number of factors about the people with whom we have to negotiate.

1.   What *kind* of people are they?

If they are our kind of people whatever that may be, we shall be more confident in knowing how to treat them. If their way of looking at the world differs markedly from our own, we have to make the effort to see their point of view.

We have to take care not to assume that they have the same outlook and perceptions of matters as ourselves.

2.   What can we learn of *their* situation and their way of looking at things?

We need to take time to *hear the story* of their situation and how they came to be negotiating with us at this time. Most of us do this when we are thinking of buying a used car from a private seller. Common sense tells us that the more we know about why the owners are selling, the better able we may be to judge whether we are wise to be doing business with them, and how many independent checks we should be making. If they have a 'good' reason to sell, which on the face of it seems plausible, we shall be reassured. If they are evasive, we shall be wary.

Once we have established for ourselves what their viewpoint may be, we do not have to agree with it or accept it. But it will surely assist us in putting over our own position.

3.   We should not presume that our emotions are the same as theirs.

We may fear certain events or situations, or feel angry or threatened by them. They may not view those events as fears at all. They may fear other events, and – moreover – may assume that we fear them too.

4. We should be wary of attributing *blame* for things that may have gone wrong and for which we hold them responsible.

In separating the people from the problem, it can be much more effective to draw attention first to *what* went wrong, rather than *whose fault* it was. This is particularly true when we ourselves may have suffered personally in some way from the failure. Attributing blame is itself judgemental, and therefore a *confrontation*. It will usually lead to some kind of *counter-move*, and in no time at all the negotiation has become adversarial again.

Referring to differences explicitly

A way of dissipating differences in perception can be to refer to them explicitly and to discuss them, provided that this can be done objectively and without attributing 'blame'. For example, 'We appreciate that you have reasons for not discussing with us the background to your wishing to sell, and we respect that. However, this makes it harder for us to make the positive assumptions that we would wish. We do not know you well, and so we are taking a risk in dealing with you. Can we now address various ways in which each of us can reassure the other, such as get an engineer's report?'

In such ways, not only does each side become more aware of the perceptions of the other, but the 'problem' – getting to a deal with which both sides feel happy – can be more easily addressed. The person is being separated from the problem, and the problem is being depersonalised.

Changing perceptions

Where we perceive that our opposite numbers have negative perceptions of us, which can impede the negotiation, we may need to consider ways of changing that perception. In addition to raising it in discussion, which may be viewed as a rather empty gesture, there is one more device that, in the right context, can be powerful. We *act* in a manner that is clearly *incompatible* with their view. If they perceive us as *shrewd and suspicious*, we might make an open gesture that implies *trust*. If, on the other hand, we are following on from a team that was viewed as *lax and easy-going*, we start *asking for proofs* and such like.

Of course, if we choose to be really astute, or devious, we might consider ways in which we can use any false perception of us to our advantage. If people feel that they are dealing with an awkward customer they may dig in their heels; or else they may soft-pedal, allowing us to make a better deal.

Our own organisation

A facet of considerable importance to remember in personal relationships with negotiators is that each one of us has to deal with our own organisation as well as with the other party. Indeed, if one thinks about it, our own organisation is likely to be with us for much longer, and in much closer relationships, than the members of the counter-party. If we do not handle our organisation right, it can prove a more persistent adversary than any outsider. For example:

(a) If we concede too much off the price, there will be a cost accountant or finance director to be reckoned with.

(b) If we offer delivery terms that cannot easily be met, the manufacturing manager will have to be mollified.

(c) If we promise quality standards that are hard to keep, there will be trouble with the production engineer.

(d) If we buy a used car that is too costly, is not comfortable and keeps breaking down, it is our spouse or partner at home who gives us a rough time about that, and for as long as we keep the car!

It is the need for each negotiating team to deal with its own people that is one of the most often overlooked features in trying to strike a deal. Indeed in confrontational negotiating, it is seldom addressed overtly at all. There is the difficulty of 'How can I 'open up' on any of these issues to the opposition without breaking faith with my own people?'. If such matters are addressed at all, it can only be with the greatest circumspection.

Effective communication

To negotiate effectively one must communicate effectively. So let us consider the essentials of communication.

First, it is necessary to *perceive the need* to communicate. Then the message itself has to be *conveyed*. It has to be *received, understood* and *accepted* so that it produces the *right actions* or *responses*.

It can be important to remember the actual processes of passing a message and getting it received.

Deciding on the means of communication

First there is the process of transmission. Let us not assume that all negotiations are conducted face to face. Many are not, and it can be wise to take time considering which medium of communication to use. A letter might be the obvious choice for a reasonably important message, and one where some record is needed. But there is a choice between first or second class; or Recorded Delivery (where proof of receipt is required); or Special Delivery (where guaranteed delivery next day is necessary); or Registered (where a financial loss results from the contents of a mislaid package). Each mode can be used to convey a different impression to the receiver, and will determine the level of attention given by the recipient.

Alternatively, we could use the fax. Faxes tend to command a higher level of priority than ordinary post. Secretaries and personal assistants may be instructed to interrupt meetings to pass faxes to recipients. Although office culture is changing, a fax generally conveys some urgency and a demand for attention. However, a fax may not be acceptable as proof of an offer of acceptance in law and, if printed on thermal paper, may have poor keeping qualities.

Some modern organisations view electronic mail (email) as they would the fax or the telephone. It is considered 'bad form' not to read one's email each day, and a response may be expected within, say, 24 hours. In such organisations there is often a measure of informality. The style may be conversational, and many of the conventions of business correspondence may be omitted. The number of emails sent and received (traffic) may be dense, such that a recipient may have several dozen incoming emails first thing in the morning, to which some kind of response is expected. Typically one can expect terse 'yes', 'no', 'I am thinking about it and will come back to you', often composed on the spot at the computer terminal. Consequently, although it may be a fast and highly convenient way of communicating certain kinds of simple, urgent message, important matters threatening legal action or termination of a business deal may best be handled in other ways. There is a danger that important emails may get missed altogether, or misconstrued, or – since it is possible only to confirm that emails have been sent successfully but not that they have been read – they may even rest in some electronic 'in-tray' for days. It may be necessary to back up such messages in other ways.

The telephone and the personal visit command attention of a different kind, and may be suitable for different kinds of message. However, it may be difficult to reach the desired recipient of our message. A secretary or PA may intercept with 'Sorry, he's in meetings all day' or 'Her diary is full all this week'.

Setting up a 'carrier wave'

We need to decide how best we might command attention so that our message is received. One approach might be borrowed from electronics. When one device is preparing to transmit to another, the first thing it does is to transmit a message giving its characteristics, and the fact that it is waiting to transmit in a certain style, at a given level of urgency and security. It does not start transmission until it receives a satisfactory response from the other end. In terms of negotiating, this suggests that a telephone call to set the scene and lay down ground rules might be a good way to start. Typically such a call might:

(a) address who we are, in terms that are crystal clear, and our subject. We might open by stating the most important benefit that the recipient stands to gain from receiving a full message from us

(b) immediately enlarge upon the benefits, to hold interest

(c) state what the other side stands to gain from continuing the dialogue

(d) summarise what he or she will lose by terminating the conversation

(e) point the way ahead

(f) invite action.

Try to hold the initiative by ensuring that the action rests with you: 'Would next Friday morning be convenient for me to come and talk to you, or would you prefer the following Tuesday?'

Other ploys, all too well-known to those who take part in telephone selling, include carefully rehearsed questions which involve the other party's participation and commitment to the discussion: 'Are you interested in a risk-free investment that will double your savings within ten years...?'

The important thing is to understand the strengths and the limitations of the medium of communication we choose. The purpose of the telephone call is NOT usually to convey the entire message, but may best be restricted merely to bringing about a situation where the full message can be conveyed later in a more suitable form.

Barriers to communication

Using a go-between

On occasion it may be possible to employ an intermediary to find out how the message was received, someone who may be respected by the 'other side', and who might actually be able to act as facilitator. The use of intermediaries in negotiating is sometimes the only way to get certain kinds of communication started. This is particularly true of governments and political parties, who cannot be seen to be 'negotiating with the enemy'; at least not until after the event, when the result has overshadowed the means. The use of *confidentiality* can be a valuable aid, and even an inducement at times.

'Noise'

As we have said, a message needs to be *conveyed, received, understood* and *accepted* so that it provokes the *right actions* or *responses*.

One factor that prevents this happening is 'noise' in the communication engineer's sense of the word: technical interference of one kind or another that may distort or totally frustrate the transmission process.

Let us consider what kinds of 'noise' there are, and how best they may be dealt with.

Interruptions

We sometimes forget that other people have interruptions as well as ourselves. These may include the unexpected arrival of the boss, the telephone, a fire alarm, a sudden change in business plans or outlook due perhaps to some action by competitors. However appropriate or important we may feel our message is, it might get totally submerged by any of these factors if they arise while we are transmitting it. As a result, our carefully constructed negotiating strategy can fall to pieces.

Overcoming noise

It is questionable whether noise will be overcome. Indeed, the risk of trying is that we may simply create more noise! Perhaps the most we can do is to manage the noise. One way to do this is to obtain 'feedback'. This involves asking the questions:

(a) Has the recipient received our message?

(b) Have we been understood?

(c) Are there any queries?

(d) Is he or she taking any action that may be consistent with their having received and accepted our message?

Sometimes a simple telephone call will achieve this. At other times the mere fact of making further contact can be dangerous. Over-eagerness to do business, for instance, might be the last message that we wish to convey in a negotiation. It is here that our intermediary can be useful.

Whenever feedback is being sought, it is useful if we can retain the initiative: not 'Can you let us know if you were happy with the proposals?', but 'We trust you were happy, and unless we hear to the contrary we shall (take some action).'

There is one more important maxim that should be remembered: 'Don't drown the message in a sea of data'.

There is a danger that, if we become too immersed in our own situation and technology, we shall obscure the message by surrounding it with too much additional information. If our message is too complex, we should consider breaking it down into easy chunks, spacing the detail over a period of time.

Matters of timing

The timing of negotiations, and the use of time in general, is a subject that crops up both in strategy and within many of the tactics. It can be crucial. Let us consider a few timing situations here, notably those that directly affect the message and its reception.

The day before the contract expires

Whether or not this is a good time to negotiate may depend upon who we are. If we are selling motor insurance, or a sole source item, and the client has a renewal coming up, it may be the ideal time. There is no chance for the prospect to go anywhere else (unless, of course, he already has!). This might be a good opportunity to renew a straightforward deal with no unusual or contentious features. Arguably, some motor insurers seek to retain existing business by deferring quotations until shortly before renewal.

If we are buyers, however, it might be a very bad time indeed. For one reason or another we appear to have left ourselves with very few options.

The day before the annual holiday

This is probably a good time if we are selling. A buyer going on leave will want to clear his desk and – other things being equal – may sign up just to achieve that result.

Just after a reorganisation

This very much depends upon who we are and what we are selling or buying. After company reorganisations, those who have survived tend to 'play it safe'. Hence it may be a bad time to offer high-risk products or services, though risk management or risk coverage products such as insurance might be high on the agenda. On the other hand, if we are talking to someone who has 'won' in the restructuring – the new boss, for instance – the opposite might apply. He may be seeking to make his mark and to change the old order of things. If we can offer goods or services that are new, dynamic and clearly a 'break with the past', the time might be just right.

On his or her birthday

Every life assurance salesman knows the answer to this one. Most of them have computer systems to ensure that neither they nor we ever forget. 'Buy before your next birthday, when the rates go up.'

Just after the buyer's promotion

The key here is to be offering something that is relevant to the new post, not the old one. In such a case, this could be a good time. The buyer will be seeking to make an impression and may not know the market. Conversely, if *we* are in the position of buyer, it may be to our advantage to talk a lot and buy very little; in effect, to keep our options open.

During a take-over battle

At such times the people at the centre tend to be totally taken up with the battle in hand, and the day-to-day running of the business tends to be on hold. This is especially true of companies defending hostile bids; rather less so in other circumstances. It is normally not a good time to negotiate any contracts involving new services. 'Due diligence' processes following an agreed bid will ensure that for a period of several weeks no one will take any risks at all. The beginning of a take-over might, however, be a very good time to sell certain services regarding shareholder relations, financial PR and other matters of that kind. Of course, if the board felt it might be accused of inactivity, it might conversely be tempted by 'a good deal'.

Upon insolvency

This depends very much upon what we are selling or buying. Many insolvencies these days are 'propped up' by legislation that attempts to encourage the survival of those parts of the business that are viable. Other parts of the business may be sold off, sometimes at attractive prices to generate cash to satisfy the creditors.

Human factors

Now let us turn to a subject that often creates more 'noise' than anything else: human factors.

Human factors

Introduction

Having specified our needs, made room for negotiation, sought to solve problems and established an effective means of communication, we need to consider the role of human factors in negotiations. First we must consider emotions.

Emotions

Human beings are subject to emotions. Key among those emotions are **joy**, **surprise**, **fear**, **doubt**, **anger** and **sorrow**.

The key to dealing with the emotions is to recognise that we do not always know when they are present. Whenever they are present, however, and whether or not they are positive influences, they are likely to *distort* our message.

Consider **joy**. It may be a very positive emotion, but nonetheless it produces unpredictability. Analytical faculties may get suspended, and cold logic overlooked.

Lottery winners are offered counselling before they sell their stories to the tabloid newspapers or give their money to the local cats' home. Hopefully, business associates are rather more in control of their emotions, but it may be counter-productive to assume that this is the case. Indeed we should never assume anything, but always attempt to find out.

'I regret to tell you that, as we have held our prices below inflation for the past five years, we have no option but to increase them by 25% for all our supplies starting next month.'

This may take the buyer completely by **surprise**. However reasonable the decision, the buyer's budgets will immediately be thrown out. His reputation with his colleagues will suffer. He may not be able to afford to accept so heavy an increase so soon. Any gratitude that he may have felt during previous years when prices were held will be forgotten. We may assume that for the remainder of that meeting very little positive dialogue will take place, and surprise may well turn to anger.

If the seller were really increasing his prices for the reason stated, he would probably have known about it, possibly subject to confirmation, some months before. A quiet warning in advance might have been sufficient to put the purchaser on his guard, to enable him to prepare, to adjust budgets and other plans, and to warn colleagues. A really astute seller might have warned of a slightly higher rise than was intended, so that when the time came he could have delivered a small but pleasant surprise. Thus the emotion would have been defused so that successful discussions could proceed.

Consider the **fear** or **doubt** caused by the following message: 'I ought to warn you that our organisation will be relocating out of the district at the end of the year, in which case we obviously will not be able to renew any of our contracts with you. Now, to examine our current proposal, if you will turn to page 16, paragraph 8 (b), line 6...'

The point about giving bad news – really bad news – to anyone is that for some while afterwards that person is unlikely to receive anything else we say to them in any meaningful sense, even though they might go through the motions of doing so. After an initial shock, the brain will be racing on other subjects:

(a) How many months' work will that leave us with?
(b) How about other customers?
(c) Will there be redundancies and shutdowns?
(d) Will I be made redundant?

If we really expect to carry on meaningful negotiations on paragraph 8, whatever it is, then we either leave it for another day or tackle it first, or deal with it in some other manner. After delivering a 'shock' message, we should assume that nothing we say will be properly received at all for some time.

Much the same situation will apply if the party we are negotiating with has just received information about some personal **sorrow**. At such times it is probably best, as well as good-mannered and tactful, to adjourn the proceedings if we possibly can. Of course, it should be realised that this could be a ploy used by the other side against us to attempt to soften our negotiating attitude

Anger is a curious emotion. Although it is part of the 'fight or flight' mechanism of primitive man, anger is to some extent an emotion most of us can control if we really want to. People can often *choose* to be angry as a way of asserting their position.

As transmitters of messages we need to consider whether anger is likely to be kindled against ourselves or against others. If against others (because we are conveying news of some third party's shortcomings), then anger might actually help us. If the third party is a competitor, for instance, and if we are bearing proof that he has short-changed our customer, we may suddenly become 'whiter than white'. Since an angry person usually has suspended their self-critical faculty, that can be the time to hit them with a 'stiff' contract. They may sign at once, just to spite the other fellow.

If the anger is directed against us, however, the reverse will apply. As astute game-players, we may need to consider where, in which direction, and with what strength our opponent's ball is going to be driven, so that we can position ourselves accordingly.

So, let us add *consider the emotions* to our checklist of things to do before we begin to negotiate.

Motivation

A facet of human behaviour that we should do well to consider is *motivation*. People are generally inclined to listen when they are motivated to hear. They are more inclined to absorb facts and opinions that confirm what they already believe. They are likely to reject or ignore that which conflicts with their beliefs.

If we are seeking to change attitudes in the course of our negotiations, much greater care will need to be given to the substance and method of presentation. People on the whole dislike *change*. It arouses the emotions of *doubt* and *fear*, according to the nature of the change. Before a person begins to accept changes and to absorb the details with any degree of commitment, he or she will need to know:

(a) *what* is changing
(b) *why* it is changing
(c) *how* they are likely to be affected.

When these matters have been addressed and absorbed, the recipient begins to become more amenable to the negotiation.

Interests, not positions

A key factor in negotiating is to conduct discussions on the basis of interests, not positions. Try always to perceive 'the law of the situation' as it has been termed.

Mary Parker Follett, one of the classic writers of this century upon management subjects, reports the case of two queues of dray men and their disputes over priorities at a loading bay. The answer lay in providing more loading points, not in a detailed negotiation between them.

Another instance involved a series of outlets for knitwear of a well-reputed brand, each bargaining with the supplier for higher priority. Shortly before an expensive computer system was engaged to programme stock allocation between up to fourteen different levels of priority, someone had the idea of reviewing factory output. By various production method improvements, it became possible to increase output so that the conflicts of priority ceased to exist.

Indeed it can be asserted that interests define the problem and its opportunities; positions expose the prejudices. Examining the interests can produce another benefit. In addition to demonstrating the points at variance between the parties, which may have to be bargained over, they also expose the common ground.

Take a typical buyer and seller relationship, for instance. The buyer may want the lowest price and the seller the highest price in each case. The buyer may be looking for quality and reliability of a standard that the seller finds no difficulty in providing, since he usually sells into a market that requires high standards. The buyer may have cash-flow problems that the seller does not have. Subject to proper safeguards, there are opportunities here for delayed payments. The buyer carries global goods-in-transit cover; the seller does not. If a deal is struck whereby carriage is at the buyer's risk, the seller may reduce the price at no effective loss to himself.

Alternatively, the buyer may need stable prices. The seller may be subject to the vagaries of changing raw material prices. Both sides might gain, however, from a long-term agreement to save respective sales and purchase costs. A long-term agreement whereby minimum purchase quantities are fixed may enable the seller to go into the market and buy his raw materials in advance so that prices may be fixed.

Examining the underlying motivations

One method of establishing interests is to ask why a particular position has been taken. Examine the forces impelling that party to hold to the position, and what might persuade him to change it. One can even draw up a form for each party in the negotiation, indicating for each position the opportunities open, and the reasons for each stance.

In doing this, of course, we shall also include ourselves. Moreover, we shall not let ourselves be misled by the presumption that there are two parties only in the negotiation. We ourselves will have colleagues and associates whose positions will influence what we can do. The other side will also have associates and colleagues. We should list them all, indicate what we feel their interests are, and relate those interests to each position or set of positions taken.

Helping people to save face

Many difficult deals could be more easily and satisfactorily concluded if the party whose expectations have had to be curtailed were given an opportunity to save face in dealing with their own organisation. It has less to do with the facts of the deal as with the manner of its expression, the terms used, the formulae applied, even the way it is announced.

It is possible to raise these emotional issues in negotiation. It is not a sign of weakness. By explaining the perceptions of other people with whom we have to deal, we make our own actions more explicable to the other participants. Correspondingly, we can encourage them to let us know about their internal situation. If we know of the forces that are constraining their attitudes to us, we may well be able to accommodate at least some of them. And provided blame or judgemental attitudes are avoided, it need not involve feelings of betrayal.

The value of small groups

In a negotiation one needs to communicate effectively in order to convey a message. With confrontational styles of bargaining, especially if many people are present, there is a danger of it degenerating into a debate. People make opposing statements partly so that others present can see that they are standing up for the home team. The other side then have to respond in kind, and of course if the media are present things can get a lot worse.

Sometimes in such cases it is necessary to break off formal open discussions and to provide for a small group of key people to meet in private. Indeed, small groups can often reach agreement far more easily than large teams. The teams are needed for their combined expertise, but it is usually possible to separate a restricted sub-set of key items on which small groups can be put to work.

How and where we sit

It can be important how teams of negotiators sit when they meet. In confrontational styles it is common for teams to sit opposite each other. This means that in human terms an actual effort has to be made by anyone seeking to strike a rapport with people on the other side, since by definition they are physically 'on the other side'.

If, as often happens, seats have been pre-arranged that way, try to find reasons to break it up. Since one cannot always refer explicitly to the reasons, it may be politic to suggest that the accountants, then the lawyers, then the sales and purchasing people from each side get together in separate groups at one stage to review different parts of the proposed agreement. Once people start working in small groups or syndicates, rapport between individuals can begin to develop. After a while it becomes emotionally as significant for 'both accountants' and 'both lawyers' to get their viewpoints accepted by the rest of the group, as for 'Team A' to prevail over 'Team B'.

Laughter, the best medicine

Remember the use of humour – a valuable if slightly unpredictable defuser of negative emotions.

Consider the following example:

Some years ago the management of an electrical factory wished to introduce more effective procedures on the shop floor, including method study and the use of the stopwatch. A meeting with shop stewards was called, to which a young consultant was invited. He was known to both sides (and 'sides' it was in that situation), having carried out most of the studies upon which the management wished to base the discussions. All the representatives filed in to the meeting-room, and took their accustomed positions on each side of the table. Somewhat cautiously, the production director outlined the plans. After a tense few moments, one of the less senior shop stewards asked the young consultant a question about the bonus scheme, which he said he found very difficult to understand. Not knowing the answer, but acting on instinct, the consultant leaned across the table and confided that he had the greatest difficulty in understanding it himself. After a second's astonished silence, there was loud laughter from the union representatives. From that moment the tension was broken, free discussion followed, and all essential points were rapidly agreed.

Too rapidly, as it happened. The stewards later had difficulty in selling the scheme to their own members. Both sides had forgotten that the stewards had an 'organisation' behind them that had to be kept content. Remember never to overlook the negotiators behind the negotiator.

Psychological factors

Now let us dig a little deeper into the psychology beneath many negotiations.

Psychological factors

Introduction

We have noted that the principled negotiator separates the people from the problem and seeks to *depersonalise* the issues. This is not to say that he or she ignores them. Negotiators are people with real feelings. Indeed those feelings often become even more accentuated in the course of negotiation, and there are many negotiations that fail merely because human reactions are not allowed for. The important point in negotiations is to use *psychological techniques* to deal with psychological situations, NOT to make *concessions* to deal with those situations.

The first point for each of us to remember is that we tend to see the world through our own perspectives. These perspectives are influenced by whatever personality factors we may possess and by our general experience of the world. All this is quite reasonable provided we remember that they are *our* perspectives. They may or may not be accurate perceptions. The second point is that, however accurate or otherwise, they may well not be the perceptions of the other side, who will have *their own* personality and environmental factors. Yet it is a human failing that we tend to *presume that others see the world and react to it as we do*. They in turn, unless they have received some training, will tend not only to view the world as they do, but to *presume that we see it in their way*. Hence there are two negative trends to be recognised and allowed for.

Various methodologies to analyse personality have been devised by psychologists and others. Let us consider some of them.

Transactional Analysis

Transactional Analysis (TA) takes as its starting point the fact that each of us communicates with one another, verbally or in some other manner, and calls such communication a 'transaction'. Moreover, the *position* that each person takes in a transaction depends on a series of recorded messages or attitudes that each of us have been absorbing since birth.

The 'Parent' mode

The first of these attitudes will have been established by our observations of the way our parents behaved towards us. Because our observations of our parents' behaviour had to be totally uncritical – since we were unable to question their world and their attitudes through lack of knowledge or awareness – 'Parent' attitudes are strong and often arbitrary in each of us. They may vary from the essential dos and don'ts to ensure *survival*: 'Don't go near the fire', 'Do eat up your food'; to *moral* attitudes: 'Don't tell lies', 'Always keep your promises'; and even tenets that many people might regard as biased or prejudiced: 'All Christians are good people', 'All Christians are bigoted', 'You can always trust a policeman', 'You can never trust a policeman'.

The truth or objectivity of such statements is immaterial for this purpose. What is of significance is that, because of the age at which we absorbed such messages, we tend to hold them in our subconscious minds, and in such a fashion that at times, and especially when under stress, they may surface and influence our attitude and behaviour in present-day situations.

That may be regarded as the judgemental side of the 'Parent' attitude. But there were other sides to our parents: the supportive, approving and nurturing sides. We have these too.

The 'Child' mode

Whilst absorbing our 'Parent' attitudes, we also built up the internal reflections of a 'Child': seeing, hearing, feeling and understanding, though entirely from our own viewpoint. As with the 'Parent', there tends to be a positive and a negative side.

On the one hand: 'I am having fun', 'I want to have fun'; and on the other, a negative rebuke or even a glance from our parent can produce the feeling: 'I am wrong. It is *my* fault.' At a young age, this can become: 'I am *totally* at fault, and always will be.' This, of course, we find devastating.

The 'Adult' mode

As the 'real' child grows older, and becomes more in control of his or her own environment, and becomes more able to perceive not merely what people tell him but what the situation really is, powers of logic gradually begin to assert themselves. This facet of personality is termed 'Adult'. The 'Adult' in our personality comprises our ability to respond to a situation in objective terms, and to use reason rather than emotion in our responses. In early years our 'Adult' is tentative and undeveloped, tending to be overshadowed by the 'Parent'.

Our world is contradictory and arbitrary. Although we develop with the three facets of 'Parent', 'Adult, and 'Child' within our personality they are often overlapping, confused and contradictory.

The four 'life positions'

In his attempt to make sense of the world in which he lives, each infant concludes that his parents, who are all-powerful, must be 'OK'. Correspondingly, because he frequently needs correction and training, and in other ways finds himself powerless and inadequate, the child often considers himself 'not OK'. Transactional Analysis concludes that even those who had happy childhoods will have reached this conclusion or position at times. As we grow up and begin to see things in perspective, those of us who become well-adjusted are able to see the world in terms of 'I am OK, you are OK', at least for most of the time.

Those who are less well-adjusted may perceive the world as: 'I am not OK, you are not OK' or 'I am OK, you are not OK' or 'I am not OK, you are OK'.

The purpose of clinical Transactional Analysis – not the concern of this book – is ultimately to enable those obsessed with any of the last three negative life positions to embrace the positive 'I am (basically) OK, the world is (basically) OK' attitude of the mature, confident adult.

The value of an understanding of Transactional Analysis in negotiation lies in the insight it can give us as to what motivates people to behave in the way they do. Well-adjusted people have elements of the 'Parent', 'Adult' and 'Child' within them in varying degrees. The difference is that, if they are truly emancipated, they are in overall control of themselves and are to a greater or lesser extent in control of their emotions even if they give way to them.

However, it has been shown that in day-to-day meetings people can 'trigger' responses from others they are dealing with, based not only upon what they say but how they say it and indeed how they behave in general. Those who 'rub us up the wrong way', whether by words or by body language, are causing us to feel for a moment 'I'm not OK, you're OK'. Since this is immediately uncomfortable for us, and bruises our ego, we may – according to our Parent/Adult/Child makeup – instantly seek to get back at them with some riposte which makes us feel 'OK' and, we imagine, will make them feel 'not OK'. In no time at all an argument will have started, often on some quite irrelevant subject. Such exchanges are known as 'crossed transactions'.

Parent/Adult/Child patterns of behaviour

Transactional Analysis shows that appropriate patterns of behaviour can be *learnt* and applied. An 'Adult' response can often deflect the negative emotions created by a 'Parental' rebuke. It can also call to order a group of people who are letting their 'Child' get out of hand, in a way which is seen to be acceptable and fair, whereas the parental 'Order!, Order!' may be taken as a rebuke. The value of knowing these techniques in a negotiating meeting can hardly be overstated.

Let us take a practical example of how Parent/Adult/Child may be perceived to operate.

Sir Winston Churchill had a lifelong regret that he had never been able to meet with his father, Lord Randolph Churchill, upon equal terms and that during his father's short lifetime he was never able to live up to his expectations and standards. There was always an unfulfilled parental 'ought' and 'should' which, in Churchill's case, acted as a spur to him to attain prominence, first on the battlefield, and later in politics and affairs of state. It was perhaps fortunate for Winston Churchill that he was able to emulate and even surpass his father in politics. Had he been unable to do this, the unfulfilled 'Parent' might have become a negative factor, as later it became for his own son Randolph. This is a problem experienced by many children of famous parents, and of others who have exacting parents who died young. Not all of them can handle it.

Winston Churchill's 'Adult' facet was – and had to be – highly developed in order to enable him to weigh logically the pros and cons of strategy. It ensured that he surrounded himself with people of ability and integrity who did not always agree with him, and it preserved him from the dangers of 'yes-man' subordinates. It warned him against flatterers and insincere people, however pleasant he might have found their company.

The 'Child' in him drove his imagination. Inspiring speeches, the use of splendid language in prose and poetry, grandiose behaviour, smoking Havanas, wearing elaborate uniforms and having fun are all facets of the 'Child'. The 'Parent' in him enabled Churchill to denounce the Nazi party in harsh, judgemental tones. The 'Adult' permitted him to be magnanimous in victory.

Parent, Adult and Child in such a man can frequently lead to internal conflict. From the accounts of those like Lord Alanbrooke, who had to deal with him, this was apparently evident in Churchill's case. Yet take away any one of the three modes, and you have a lesser individual.

Consider what all this may mean in negotiating. Not everyone has Parent, Adult and Child in balance, or to the same degree, but by studying their dominant facets of personality we can learn their susceptibilities. Examine the following:

Parent attitudes

Must, must not; should, should not; the 'right way' to do things ('all other ways are wrong!'); the frown, the furrowed brow; the wagging of heads; the pointing of index fingers; the saying of 'tut tut'; the use of expressions such as 'If you want *my* advice' (and then giving it), 'If I were you...'; always, never – judgemental and condescending words and gestures, or an attitude of mind that holds to these positions, whether or not such expressions are actually used, are all typical of a Parent attitude. The word 'patronising' comes from the same root as 'parent' or 'father'.

Adult attitudes

The use of logical language: what, when, who, why, how?; 'It is my opinion that... something is true' rather than an outright statement that it *is* true (in circumstances that allow room for debate); the absence of emotion; and attention to the matter in hand without bias or undue involvement are all signs of an Adult attitude.

Child attitudes

'I wish', 'I want', 'I don't care'; tears, laughter, the shrugging of shoulders; the use of superlatives in language such as biggest, best, highest; a determination to impress the 'Parent' within, or to put it in its place, or to ignore it, are all giveaway signs of a Child attitude.

Parent/Adult/Child negotiating

It may be easiest to consider Parent/Adult/Child negotiating if we relate it to the marketing or selling of a well-understood consumer product such as a motor car.

> The Adult in us has learnt that there are various logical factors involved in choosing and buying a car. There is the need: how large is our family, do we need the car for business or pleasure or both, how much can we afford to spend, and what is the likely annual mileage? This line of reasoning will lead us into fuel consumption, rates of depreciation, interest on any loans

we may need and so on. It will tell us whether we need a two-door, or a four-door saloon, or a hatchback, or an estate car. It may remind us that the maximum permitted speed in this country is 70 miles an hour, and cause us to consider whether we really need all the acceleration that a powerful model would give us.

Then the vehicle salesman takes over. He knows all about the Child in us. We shall be shown glossy brochures. There will be elaborate choices of colour and style to be considered. We shall be offered convertibles, models with air conditioning, sleek styling, spoilers. Suddenly we realise that it would be rather nice to have one of the flashier models. We have seen them around on the motorways, being driven by rather smart, upwardly mobile-looking people. Indeed, some of our wealthier neighbours or more successful colleagues at work may drive them. And then there is the question of the latest number plate, or even a personalised one incorporating our initials or nickname or some other gimmick. By this time logic has become a background issue. Our minds are set upon impressing our associates; in our imagination we are driving into the company car park, or the forecourt of our local inn, exchanging banter about our splendid new acquisition.

The salesman hasn't finished, of course. He is well aware of our Adult lurking in the background. Out will come warranty brochures, inclusive memberships of the RAC or the AA, first year insurance cover, and such like. And so it goes. Usually the last thing to be mentioned is the price.

But what of our Parent in all these proceedings? Much depends upon the parental programming to which we are subject. Often it may get subordinated for the time being to the needs of the Child. In these cases it may reassert itself later – typically in the 'cooling off period' that the law allows for certain classes of sales transaction. On occasion it can take on a supportive or nurturing voice: 'You've worked hard for that car. You *deserve* it.' More often it may be cautionary or reproving: 'That's *far* too much to spend', or 'It's much too risky'; 'Save for a rainy day' or even 'You ought to be taking far more exercise. Buy a bicycle instead!'.

Of course it can be argued that our Child will be satisfied and assuaged by driving a flashier car, such that it will be more confident and more adult in future. With such arguments does our Child 'negotiate' with our Parent.

The point to note is that whereas the Adult is a logical position, both Parent and Child are emotional: 'I ought' or 'I want'. Yet each demand a measure of recognition or satisfaction if the individual is to conclude the negotiation happy with the deal that has been struck.

A well-adjusted individual is *not* one who is totally adult. Indeed, it was once suggested that a total Adult would be 'the kind of guy who'd marry Audrey Hepburn – for her money!' A truly well-adjusted individual can be described as, one who:

1. has learnt to recognise the Child in him, its likes, fears and methods of expressing itself

2. understands the Parent within, its motivations, admonitions, and how they came to be there

3. is sensitive to the three facets in others, particularly the Parent which has to do with others' egos and self-respect.

In our own lives we should always remember to 'stop and count up to ten', in order to give the Adult a chance to analyse the often-conflicting data and emotions that may come to the fore during a negotiation.

It should be mentioned that within Transactional Analysis the terms 'Parent', 'Adult' and 'Child' are regarded as technical terms that have specified meanings among the practitioners of this technique. They are *not* meant to be equated to our real parents, or our actual selves as children, or even as real adults. They are merely a way of analysing and studying aspects of the personality.

Transactional Analysis of corporations

Some authorities hold that corporations as well as individuals can be analysed into Parent, Adult and Child dominance. Be that as it may, it can certainly be helpful in planning to bargain with a company to reflect upon its culture and the likely effect that this will have upon its negotiators.

Paternalistic or parent companies

Parent companies are hierarchical. Power resides at the top. Discipline is strict, and there are many rules and operating procedures. Less senior staff are viewed as 'children'. Children are assumed to be wayward and irresponsible by their nature. In such companies expressions such as 'staff have to be managed' will be heard. It is assumed that everyone has to have a manager, and that managing is all about telling people what to do and making sure that they do it.

Parent managements do consider that they have certain responsibilities, however. Those who obey the rules are seen as loyal. Loyalty is highly regarded, often more so than ability, which over a period can make such companies vulnerable. Disloyalty (which can include acting or speaking out of turn) tends to be heavily punished. This can include expulsion from the 'family'. Though 'father' is unwilling to do this to his 'sons', he will not hesitate if he considers that the 'family' has been compromised. Typically, a redundant executive from such a company is expurgated from the company 'language' and never mentioned again in memos or documentation, much like the black sheep who has been deported.

Junior staff in such organisations tend after a while to behave like children, as they are expected to do. Corporate practical jokers will emerge – especially on the factory floor if there is one, since these are the people furthest from 'grace' in a strict hierarchy. Some of these pranks can be quite serious, dangerous and expensive. No one is ever caught, of course, though unofficially many people know who the pranksters are and secretly applaud them as 'kings of the playground'.

Top management takes all this as confirmation that junior staff or works personnel are 'children', and redoubles its efforts to supervise and control them, with carrots and with big sticks. The executives, the more senior 'children', will in part be rewarded with a lot of child-oriented, status symbol rewards, to which great internal importance will be given: the exact size and type of company car, the size of office, how many squares of carpet one is allowed for one's rank, which washroom one may use.

Negotiating teams from such companies will reflect this culture. Even if individual members of the teams are Adult-dominated, back at base they will have to appear parental in negotiating style. Whatever agreements are reached, an important element will be structuring matters so that the negotiating team do not lose face, and if possible gain prestige.

Adult companies

The Adult, we have to remember, is totally logical, with virtually no emotion. As a result, there are not too many truly Adult companies because most people are not like that and ultimately do not fit into such organisations. Those companies that are Adult tend to pass through an Adult phase, after which they modify their culture to something a little less extreme.

Adult companies are totally oriented towards the needs of the tasks in hand. There is little or no hierarchy, and very few status symbols. They lend themselves to network management. People grab offices, supporting staff and services whenever they can demonstrate that they need them. They also grab high salaries *at that time* because for the moment they are indispensable. There is high commitment to the job, and a high degree of flexibility. Success in the job means success in personal and corporate terms. People as individuals are of little account, and human resources departments, if they exist at all, are of relatively little influence and exist mainly to execute routine personnel functions and to ensure legal compliance. Such companies behave ruthlessly towards failure, as there is little concept of the company as 'father' with bonds of loyalty to 'children' who have tried hard. An executive who falls down on the job is likely to arrive and find there is no office for him, and no work one day. It has been given to someone else. He may be left to conclude that he might as well leave. Such companies tend to find themselves before tribunals under 'constructive dismissal' claims.

After a while some of the more successful members of the company may conclude that a more stable base is desirable – possibly because of customer complaints about staff turnover, or because able people leave to find greater security – and the culture is modified. Negotiating with the Adult company tends to be negotiating with the man of the moment. If we have a product or service they want right now and if the conditions are right they will buy. On the whole we can forget about long-term commitments, loyalty bonuses, building up relationships of trust and so on, *unless* such things are relevant to the current or foreseeable order book.

Child companies

True Child companies, like Adult companies, cannot exist on their own for too long. The child will do what it wants to do and what it finds interesting.

Child-oriented organisations are often engaged in pure research or 'state-of-the-art' development. They may employ highly talented people who are there mainly for the love of the work, not for the status. Business needs can be perceived as partly irrelevant in the pursuit of knowledge or science for its own sake, and there lies the problem.

One such organisation was cynically described as having as its mission statement 'To provide interesting work for the chaps to do at least cost to the shareholder'. As long as the 'lads' are producing really useful products and ideas of marketable value, such companies can subsist. They tend to be very friendly and happy places, with a lot of trust and mutual respect.

Unless there is careful direction, however, with an Adult or two strategically placed where it matters, the risk is that Child companies either fail or get absorbed into another body at the behest of owners or shareholders who have lost patience.

Changing modes

What usually happens in practice is that company cultures change over the years. An Adult company may become less intolerant and 'short-term', thus taking on some of the characteristics of the Parent – though usually without most of the trappings of power and hierarchy. A Child company becomes more Adult in order to survive. The Parent company finally realises that it no longer has any innovative, creative staff; to survive, it absorbs a Child or an Adult company with products or bright ideas, and consequently has to modify some of its own attitudes. The result of much of this is that corporations above a certain size will have 'pockets' of all three cultures to some degree. In planning to bargain with them, it pays to take time to ascertain which culture one is dealing with, and to what degree. Some of this may come to light only during the negotiation, but a general appreciation of Transactional Analysis can help a negotiating team define what the real motivating factors are on the other side of the table.

Summing up on Transactional Analysis

Transactional Analysis can be a convenient way for the layman in matters of psychology to sum up, quickly, the personality types in a negotiation, both the individuals and the corporate cultures in which they are operating. It can help to explain some of the apparently illogical patterns of behaviour that some of us display all of the time, and all of us display some of the time. Usually we cannot change the Parent, Adult or Child positions of others by analysis. What we can do, however, is to recognise the negative or 'crossed' day-to-day transactions that are occurring all around us as we negotiate. On the whole, uncrossed or positive transactions, even the rather immature Parent-to-Child ones, contribute to the feelings of 'I am OK', which at least put the participants into a relaxed positive frame of mind. One can communicate with people when they are in that situation. Negative or 'crossed' transactions, on the other hand, assault the ego. They give rise to 'I am not OK' feelings, which may trigger a gut reaction along the lines of 'Oh yes I am OK, he's the one who is not OK'. Insecure people have often learnt that anger or hate is a preferable emotion to fear, and they will display it instinctively. As negotiators we can of course choose how we use this analysis, but we need to remember that crossed transactions will often inhibit logical thought and communication.

Anyone who wishes to apply the principles of Transactional Analysis needs to study the subject properly. These paragraphs are merely an overview. Possibly the best-known book on the subject is *I'm OK, You're OK* by Thomas A. Harris MD, available in paperback from most business bookshops. A related subject, that of the psychological 'games' that people play upon one another to preserve or enhance their egos, is covered in another paperback, *Games People Play* by Eric Berne, who is generally regarded as the founder of Transactional Analysis.

Neurolinguistic programming (NLP)

Another technique that has been developed over the last two decades, and which can be useful for analysing personality types in negotiating is neurolinguistic programming, known as NLP[1]. Like many of these techniques, NLP originated in California. It was developed by a linguist, John Grinder, and a mathematical programmer, Richard Bandler. They sought to explain in mathematical or logical ways how the mind works, by bringing together numerous existing known methods and augmenting them by their own observed research into what makes us 'tick'.

Part of NLP has to do with re-programming one's mind and impulses in order to maximise positive thinking. Top athletes and tennis players have used it with success. As such it may be considered a 'life skill', much like negotiating itself. Its relevance to us, however, is as another way of analysing personality types and ways of thinking and behaving.

Three dimensions

According to NLP, each of us has three different axes or dimensions to our thought processes.

Visual

To a greater or lesser extent we think in pictorial terms. We remember experiences in terms of how they looked at the time. We recall our own homes and the homes of our friends by their outward appearance, so that if we leave our address book at home we are not necessarily lost, unless we are seeking a place where we seldom go.

Auditory

To a greater or lesser extent we remember sounds: the sound of people's voices, the sound of machinery, the sound of music. Some of us who are commuters find that we subconsciously memorise the sound of familiar railway lines and wheel beats. Even the deepest sleep in the train home after a day's work will not prevent our minds from jerking us awake as the train crosses a known set of points when we approach our destination. 'Play it again, Sam' we may say, relying on music to revive emotions or memories much deeper than the notes of the piano. Or 'Listen, darling, they're playing *our* tune!'

Sensory

To a greater or lesser extent we remember the touch, smell or taste of things associated with places, people or circumstances. Sometimes a fragrance, inhaled many years afterwards, can bring vividly to mind not only an event, but the emotions we felt at that time. The smell of fresh paint may remind us immediately of a house we moved into as a child, and where we were very happy, or possibly very sad. Lavender may bring to mind a garden we once knew and loved, or a relative who used lavender scent. An entire industry has been built upon the profound effects of smell and its associations, as is witnessed by the vast range of perfumes and aftershaves available.

NLP holds that, whereas some of us may use visual, auditory and sensory dimensions in our thoughts or communications to more or less the same extent, one or two of these three channels are dominant in most people. This gives us both a problem and an opportunity.

The problem is, as always, that we tend to assume that the rest of the world is like us. If we express ourselves in terms of word pictures we shall be less than effective in communicating to people who are auditory, much as a musician may be less moved by an old master than by a symphony. If we are predominantly sensory, and pride ourselves upon our open, warm reception of people on a physical level ('I cannot stand people who have a weak handshake!'), we may find we are physically repellent to others for whom enthusiastic physical contact is a 'turn off', an unwanted intrusion into their private space.

Reading the signs

The opportunity this gives us is, of course, the chance to study techniques such as NLP and learn how to turn people 'on', in perfectly acceptable ways. NLP practitioners' analysis suggests that there is quite a vocabulary of attitudes that may tell us how their minds are working.

When someone looks **upwards and to the right**, they are likely to be constructing an imaginary scene – 'Just imagine when these negotiations are over and I can be off sailing on my yacht'.

Upward and to the left is a recollection of a scene from their memory – 'Last year at this time I was in Greece', for instance.

Sideways to the right indicates a *constructed sound* – the boss congratulating him on a successful negotiation, something which hitherto may never have happened.

Sideways left indicates a *remembered sound*, such as a favourite piece of music.

Looking downwards and to the right may indicate feelings or internal emotions, be they confidence or uncertainty.

Looking downwards and to the left suggests *internal dialogue* – 'I must get a grip on these discussions, or we shall make more concessions than I can live with. What shall I say next?'.

Looking straight ahead, defocused, indicates a remembered or constructed image of some kind.

'It's only daydreaming', we may say, and yet we all do it. A key to what others may be thinking in negotiation can be very valuable indeed. There are in fact numerous figures of speech in our language that support these hypotheses. 'Things are *looking up*'. 'I am *feeling down*'. 'You *look down* in the mouth today'. 'That man makes me *downright furious*'. 'I *see* where you're coming from'. 'I *hear* you'.

Of significance is the challenge 'Pay attention. Look at me when I'm speaking to you!' So long as we have total eye contact with that other person, the most we can achieve is to receive the spoken word. It is not until we look away that we begin to digest the words, their meaning and their significance.

In negotiating, we can begin to recognise the three predominant types by the language they tend to use. A *visual person* will 'see' the point of an argument. He or she will 'focus' upon problems. He may take a 'dim view' of something he disapproves of, but 'the picture will be bright' if he is able to win the argument.

The *auditory person* will 'hear us loud and clear'. They will 'tell' us exactly what they want us to 'hear'. They may have to 'talk' to their colleagues about our suggestions. They may be reluctant to make 'snap' decisions, especially when the unexpected suddenly comes 'bang' at them.

Someone to whom other senses are predominant may tell us that something in our argument does not 'feel' right to them. They like management to make an 'impact' upon events, but when things go wrong it certainly 'leaves a bad smell'. They will, however, be prepared to take the 'rough with the smooth', even though this may leave a 'bitter taste'.

Negotiating in teams – the Belbin team types

Some negotiations have to be carried out by individuals working on their own. However, research shows that, over a period at least, group solutions tend to be more effective than individual solutions. For a team to be effective it needs to have a common goal or focus. To be fully effective it needs to become greater than the sum of its individual members.

Dr Meredith Belbin, researching initially at the Henley Management Centre, analysed the characteristics of nine essential team roles. Arguably, to get the most effective team of negotiators, one needs to have each of the nine represented in it. Fortunately for those who have small teams, it is possible to combine more than one characteristic within each individual, since as with most personality scoring there are seldom absolutes. So what are these nine characteristic types?

The Coordinator or 'Chairman'

This characteristic is represented by an individual who is not a particularly critical thinker or analyser. He is dominant, though not aggressive. He trusts other people, and he regards them as providers of resources, and not as threats. He has a high regard for duty, for doing things properly and 'by the book'. His concern is for practicality rather than innovative or creative thinking, and this type of individual does not over-respond to pressure brought upon him by others. Outwardly he can appear enthusiastic, but internally he is careful and objective. Originally termed 'Chairman', this personality is typified by the kind of person who gets chosen for the detached, calm, unbiased role in a group. If he takes the chair, as he often may, it is as the unbiased conductor of business in a proper manner, not the dynamic 'chairman, chief executive and dominant leader' of the group. The character tends to work better as *primus inter pares,* among near equals, rather than as director of subordinates. This personality is liable to clash with Shapers.

The 'Shaper'

The true Shaper is a dynamic contributor to a group and therefore valuable. He strives to get his ideas across, likes action and quick results, and prefers it when there are willing supporters in the team. He has a high degree of nervous energy and creative tension, and dislikes formal constraints such as rules and procedures. A shaper can be impatient and intolerant, and is liable to be compulsive about pet theories. A Shaper wants to 'make it happen', and for that reason can be a good team leader. He doesn't mind taking unpopular decisions, or upsetting political apple carts if he feels it is necessary to get results.

The Innovator

The Innovator is an ideas person. Usually with a high IQ, the Innovator has self-confidence (sometimes more so than the Shaper) but may have a problem with uninhibited expression. Ideas are more important to him than people. The Innovator is a very useful team member to have participate in brainstorming and related activities but is not an 'organisation man', so that if your organisation is highly structured and hierarchical you may have difficulty in finding an Innovator. An Innovator is not always practical, so may need to have his ideas tempered by others in the team. The term 'Innovator' was originally termed 'Plant'. Like all these personality type terms, however, it can be dangerous to relate dictionary definitions to them. An 'Innovator' for this purpose may be defined as someone who, having taken a specified personality test, has scored high on a sub-set of questions designed to reveal personality traits that we have decided to call 'Innovator'.

The Monitor or Evaluator

This team member is a good evaluator and 'devil's advocate'. He is serious, cautious and objective. He quite enjoys 'knocking' others' ideas, and may appear superior and even supercilious. He is a member of the team to be kept well under control during brainstorming sessions, but to be let loose later upon the 'bright ideas' to help sort the wheat from the chaff. The Monitor or Evaluator is meticulous in 'getting it right every time', and in certain high-risk negotiations can be an essential colleague.

The Implementor

Something of an 'organisation man', the Implementor works within procedures cultures and ways of doing things. A practical translator of theory into practice, the Implementor is unhappy with quick changes, expediency and adaptability. A reliable logician, he may have leadership potential, but may be less effective in situations that are fluid and that call for imagination and flexibility.

The Team Worker

A seeker after harmony and concord, the Team Worker has a high concern for the feelings and well-being of the group. He may not be particularly tough or decisive, but is a good delegator. He can hold the team together, but in a quiet way for which due credit may not always be given.

The Resource Investigator

The Resource Investigator is people-oriented. He has a restless, enquiring attitude to life and has a wide range of contacts. He is positive and tends to be impulsive and may drop one task for another if it interests him more. The Resource Investigator seeks variety and challenge, and is not so much an 'ideas' person as one who stimulates others to raise ideas. This is often his value to the team. He needs to be kept focused upon the essentials in hand. The Resource Investigator can be a good negotiator.

The Completer or Finisher

This personality type tends to be somewhat tense, and has a compulsive desire to finish things off to perfection. A good 'detail' person, keen on getting things done on schedule, the Completer may get on other people's nerves from time to time. Perversely, an extreme 'Completer' can operate *against* getting things finished, since to get them properly finished can involve perpetual refinement and improvement. He is not a good delegator, since no one can fully measure up to his own standards of 'finish'.

The Specialist

This personality type lays stress upon acquiring specialised knowledge or skill. He is keen on developing and defending his own chosen area of knowledge. He has great pride in what he is doing, but relative disinterest in other people's areas. Not many people have the commitment to become truly effective Specialists, but those who do can be invaluable. In leadership roles they command a good deal of respect because no one else knows their subject like they do. As a result, decisions based upon their knowledge tend to be correct ones.

Establishing Belbin

To establish Belbin roles properly, everyone needs to take brief personality tests and have the resultant scores analysed professionally. This may be expensive but, if the outcome of impending negotiations is to be worth many millions of pounds, it could be argued that Belbin comes cheap.

In such analysis (which does not take long), there are no 'right' or 'wrong' results. It is about self-knowledge and an understanding of others in the group. Analysis features applying one's own personal weightings to such statements as 'I enjoy analysing situations in my work', and 'I enjoy the social side of working relationships'. Self-scoring is done at the end of the exercise, and there is a certain amount of mixing of statements, so that one is not particularly conscious of where a given line of response is going to lead. The greatest value in applying this technique is when it can be done with the whole negotiating team present and involved. There are three reasons for this.

1. Few of us emerge as a single personality type. Most of us have a dominant type among the nine, with two or more subsidiary types, representing alternative roles that we would be quite well able to assume where the situation demanded it, and to a greater or lesser extent according to the scoring. It can be useful to have professional help in interpreting such matters.

2. It can be useful for each member of a team to know the personality types not only of himself but of others with whom he will be

conducting negotiations. The team coordinator might care to keep an inventory of such matters.

3. It can serve to remind the team, and its overall convenor or leader, that it can be valuable to pass control of the group from one member to another during the course of a negotiation, much like the lineout of three-quarters in a game of rugby football.

The team that is always operating under the domination of one leader can usually be outmanoeuvred by a flexible team on the other side. We might open with our Coordinator/Chairman type dominating and then the lead might pass to one or more Shapers in the group whilst ideas are being developed. In the final analysis we could have a Specialist who might either have a legal or technical training. Such a person could assume command when final details are being hammered out, to be quickly replaced by our Coordinator in the event of deadlock. Sometimes all this will happen instinctively. However, it can be better when it is *planned*.

There are other facets to the Belbin analysis system that call for specialist interpretation. Each type tends to possess certain weaknesses in team activity, as an inherent characteristic. It can be helpful to know what these are, and the intensity with which they may show themselves under stress. A full negotiating team inventory will list:

1. natural roles
2. roles that can be assumed
3. roles better avoided
4. tendencies to weakness that may have to be allowed or 'lived with'.

A triangular analysis

One method of personality analysis views people under three types: the 'sturdy battler', the 'friendly helper' and the 'logical thinker'. The characteristics of each of these are listed below.

The Sturdy Battler

The Battler lives in a perceived world of striving and strife, of targets to be fought for and achieved, of power to be obtained. He will initiate matters, press for results, and is highly task-oriented. In looking at others, what is significant to the Battler is their strengths or their weaknesses, and who is winning and who is losing. He will seek to dominate by giving orders, by issuing threats and offering challenges. This personality is power-oriented, and his main fear is that power will be lost. The world is full of people who are 'for us' who will be wholeheartedly supported as long as the perceived support remains, and those who are 'agin us' who must be ruthlessly removed at all costs. There is suspicion and possibly contempt for those who are seen as 'soft' or 'sentimental'. Rules or principles may be perceived as bendable or stretchable in their interpretation in order to reach a given target. A Sturdy Battler might be highly effective in selling or team management. Someone who scores very high indeed on this scale, however, may become the 'super salesman' who always 'brings home the bacon' in tough situations but who is almost unmanageable within the organisation or the team because of his ruthless manipulative inclinations.

The Friendly Helper

This character lives in a world of harmony and goodwill, even of affection. Instinctively he will harmonise, even to the point of making concessions or compromises. He will express concern for people, by encouragement and warmth. He views others in terms of who is warm and who helps others, in contrast to those who antagonise or cause hurt. His fear is of not being liked or of being overwhelmed by a hostile atmosphere. Someone scoring moderately on this scale can be a valuable team member because of the encouragement he offers. It used to be said that every team needs a 'Well done !' person as well as a 'What the blazes!' person, and the Helper's role here is clearly that of the encourager. An extreme high scorer on this scale can be dangerous in some circumstances, since he will tend to have total concern for people and their feelings to the exclusion of getting things done.

The Logical Thinker

The Logical Thinker is an introvert, whereas the other two personalities tend to be more or less outgoing. The Thinker lives in a world of logic, of gathering knowledge, and of critically evaluating every choice before deciding what to do. Other people are judged in terms of who is bright and who is stupid; who are clear thinkers and who are 'wafflers'. The Thinker tends to be a dark horse, a chess player, or a poker player who does not reveal his hand. He is not too bothered about helping others unless it suits his scheme of things. Some people on this scale are cynically referred to by colleagues as the 'black holes' of the workplace. They will absorb as much information or assistance as they can get but they do not volunteer much in return. If you want something from them, you have to ask, and sometimes chase or negotiate. Pitted against the other two types, the Thinker will probably win in the long run, unless the culture of the organisation is against him.

Plotting the triangle

Analysis of these types can be conducted by inviting answers to 'What would you do if' questions. Some practitioners in this triangular analysis portray the results upon three spokes of a wheel, so that extreme scorers are near the outer circumference, whereas low scorers are near the centre or hub. As with all such systems, most us score some marks on each of the three dimensions. Those who fall around the centre are sometimes termed 'Hubs'. 'Hubs' of all three types are often regarded as the run of the mill, fairly well-rounded and adjusted, essential individuals without whom few teams could operate. They are the cement that holds all the extremists together.

Further refinements can include re-running the questionnaires on the basis of 'What would you do if... in circumstances where you are under pressure, stress or anxiety?' The results may indicate that a natural Friendly Helper, for instance, may veer towards one of the other personality types when threatened.

Sometimes it can be perceived that particular levels of management in an organisation tend to be executives of a certain type. Section managers may be Sturdy Battlers, division managers above them might be Logical Thinkers, whereas at board level there might be a measure of Friendly Helpers, commanding loyalty and respect and holding things together but relying upon the other levels to solve many of the 'tough' problems for which they will be more fitted. More often, however, it will be one of the other two types that subsists at the very top.

When negotiating it can be helpful to have a 'feel' for these stratas of personality. Often it can be politic to pair off negotiators by level of seniority, so that technicians bargain over detail, and directors finally meet to resolve outstanding matters of principle or to resolve deadlocks. To know whether we are likely to deal with Sturdy Battlers or Logical Thinkers can be useful in deciding which of our own people shall represent us.

The Myers-Briggs Personality Type Indicator

Based upon a practical and simplified interpretation of the theories of Carl Jung, the Myers-Briggs Type Indicator was developed by researcher Isabel Briggs-Myers around the time of World War 2, continuing work begun by her mother, Katherine Cook Briggs. The Indicator identifies four scales or dimensions of personality upon which an individual lies.

The scale of Extrovert or Introvert

Peter Myers, in his book *Gifts Differing*, gives this example: to a total Extrovert, 'Hell at a party' means not being able to get there, perhaps because one has not been invited; to the Introvert it means having to endure it when you are there.

The scale of how we perceive things

We may perceive things by using our five senses (seeing, hearing, feeling, smelling, tasting) or by using our intuition (a hunch, an instinctive response).

The scale of how we judge things

This includes thinking logically or objectively about an issue versus feeling subjectively about it.

The scale of perceiving or judging

When we are studying a new subject with an open mind, we are perceiving. When our mind has been made up, we are judging. A predominantly 'judging' person tends to lead a more ordered life than one who is dominantly 'perceiving'. There is the difference between those who see everything as black or white and those who can perceive varying shades of grey.

Clearly there is a place for each end of each scale, though most perfectly well-adjusted individuals will be not wholly at one end or the other of these dimensions. However, we are dealing here with *dominant inclinations* like being left-handed or right-handed. As with all such systems there is no right or wrong, good or bad, normal or abnormal.

Auxiliary positions

Having now identified eight different *dominant* positions or processes (one at each end of four scales), Myers-Briggs then introduces the concept of there being one other position that is said to be *auxiliary*. Hence a well-balanced Introvert can nonetheless practise an auxiliary process for dealing with social skills. Parties do not have to be 'sheer hell', but merely a less preferred way of making contact with people. The Introvert may rather do this in one-to-one meetings, but has enough small talk to 'get by' at parties when necessary. The well-balanced Extrovert prefers to be outgoing, but has enough auxiliary 'savvy' to know when to keep quiet.

Since each personality has an auxiliary position on each scale as well as a dominant position, this gives rise to a four by four matrix of sixteen combinations. The whole matter becomes quite intricate, because whereas the Extrovert tends to display his or her dominant positions in dealing with the outside world, the Introvert tends normally to display the auxiliary positions.

Myers likens it to visiting two army generals encamped in the field of battle. Each general is the *dominant* position, and each one has an aide-de-camp, the *auxiliary*. When we visit the Extrovert we always talk to the general himself. He comes out of the tent to meet and to deal with us. His aide-de-camp stays in the background, or even disappears completely into the tent. When we visit the Introvert the opposite is true. It is the auxiliary, the aide-de-camp, who comes out of the tent to meet and deal with us. The 'real' general remains inside the tent dealing with matters of utmost importance to him, and the aide is there in front to ward off interruptions. Only for matters of real importance, or when the friendship is close, do visitors get to meet the Introvert general.

People who do not realise this can totally misjudge or underestimate the Introvert. They perceive the aide-de-camp as if he were the general himself, whereas the hidden general far outranks the personality that appears on the surface, and is different from it.

There are many examples, particularly in show business, but also in other kinds of business, of the Introvert cloaking his true personality under a highly successful auxiliary persona, his 'act'. Until we have understood the act we have not begun to understand the Introvert.

Doctor: 'You're suffering from depression; go and see Coco the Clown.'

Patient: 'But I a m Coco the Clown.'

The eight Myers-Briggs type indicators are sometimes coded as listed below.

E Extrovert	Those who tend to talk first, think later.
I Introvert	Those who rehearse before they act.
S Sensing	Those who like precise answers to precise questions.
N Intuitive	Those who think about several subjects at once; like puzzle-solving.
T Thinking	Those who are cool and calm in a crisis; concern for truth before popularity.
F Feeling	Those who lay stress upon taking the feelings of others into account.

J Judging	Those who thrive on order: 'A place for everything, and everything in its place'.
P Perceiving	Those who are creative, spontaneous, easily distracted; their desks are seldom tidy.

One text upon the subject even has the combinations categorised as follows, in terms of how they might appear within a business organisation.

ISTJ	Life's natural organisers
ISFJ	Committed to getting the job done
INFJ	An inspiring leader and follower
INTJ	Life's independent thinkers
ISTP	'Just do it!'
ISFP	Actions speak louder than words
INFP	Making life kinder and gentler
INTP	Life's problem-solvers
ESTP	Making the most of the moment
ESFP	Let's make work fun
ENFP	People are the product
ENTP	Progress is the product
ESTJ	Life's natural administrators
ESFJ	Everyone's trusted friend
ENFJ	Smooth-talking persuaders
ENTJ	Life's natural leaders

Myers-Briggs analyses the characteristics of each of the sixteen positions or combinations in some depth. There is relevance in choice of occupation, performance, choice of colleagues or team memberships to provide complementary traits, and analysis in depth as to what each grouping has to gain or to lose from each other grouping, and how best it can be used in team-building.

---

[1] *NLP at Work* by Sue Knight (Nicholas Brealey publishing 1995) and *Type Talk at Work* by Kroeger and Thuesen (Dell Paperback 1992).

Getting our act together

Introduction

We have already suggested that the single most important step to effective negotiation is to prepare for it. Let us now consider the various actions that we might take.

First analysis of needs

We should begin by making a list. Typically we might specify the need we have, the product or service that we wish to buy or sell, the reason we are dealing with the outside world, and why we cannot fill our need internally. Our list might look like this:

1. What is the purpose of our negotiation?

2. What do we want to achieve?

3. What set of results would represent a successful outcome?

4. What kinds of result would represent those that we can live with if we have to?

5. What kind of a deal would be so bad that we might wish that we had never begun to negotiate in the first place?

Having drawn up our list of needs we need to ask ourselves what this tells us about (a) the other party or parties with whom we may negotiate and (b) about ourselves, our colleagues and our own organisation.

The other party or parties

Again, drawing up a list of questions to consider may be useful.

1. Is there one other party to this negotiation, or is this a deal in which three or four parties collaborate? If the latter, it may be necessary to consider each party in turn as a separate entity.

2. What do we know of their objectives or needs?

3. What else can we find out? For instance, do we know who their directors are? What do they buy or sell?

4. How sound are they financially?

5. Are they expanding or contracting?

6. Do we have a copy of their latest report and accounts?

7. Do we have someone available to us who is able to evaluate such things?

8. Have there been public announcements on them, perhaps by the Stock Exchange or in the national or local press?

9. Do we have access to a press cuttings service to keep us informed about them? If not, is our business with them sufficiently important to set one up?

10. Has our research told us anything which might help us to build up a profile of them, and how they might be expected to behave in discussions with us?

11. What is the history of our own involvement with them?

12. Have we, or anyone else in our organisation or whom we know, negotiated with them before?

13. Did we find them 'fair', 'soft' or 'tough'?

14. How did they conduct talks? Did they field a team or send a single representative?

15. Were they flexible or rigid?

16. Did they provide contract terms, or leave that to us?

17. If they did provide contract terms, were those terms appropriate for the work in hand, or 'our standard boiler plate, take it or leave it'? If the latter, did we concede? If not, how did the negotiation end?

18. Are they known to be good at planning, or is everything needed in a hurry? If the latter, we might use that knowledge to advantage. For instance, we might offer a high-speed delivery service for our goods at premium rates. On the other hand, if we are buyers, we might consider

pressing for a 'time of the essence' undertaking, or heavy penalties for delay.

19. What emphasis do they place upon quality? Is it important to them in their business, and how are we placed – if we are supplying – to meet those standards?

20. On the other hand, if we are receiving goods or services, how does their perceived quality match up with our requirements?

Our own organisation

It has been observed that successfully negotiating with our own organisation is a key yet underestimated part of reaching a satisfactory outcome. Let us consider who might be involved, what manner of people they are, and what interests they may represent.

1. What is the profile of our organisation?

2. Who owns it?

3. Who are the key decision-makers?

4. Are we in direct touch with them? If not, what can we deduce about them and their objectives?

5. Are we a profit-making entity, a philanthropic institution or a service function?

6. What are our overall objectives?

7. What can we learn about our organisation? The time to make certain we know what makes our organisation tick is in *advance* of talks with another party – not halfway through.

Let us now consider each of the main functions of our organisation in turn.

Our public profile

1. What kind of a profile do we have?

2. Are we well-known in the world at large, within our own market or are we a small organisation known only to those with whom we do business or whom we contact?

3. Does our profile influence the negotiation we are about to commence?

4. Is that influence beneficial, or a hindrance?

5. If it is a hindrance, are there any steps we can take to mitigate the effects, and so 'free us up' at the negotiating table?

Advantages and disadvantages of size

One very small organisation in the Information Technology field uses its membership of a reputable networking association as a selling point to mitigate the effects of size when tendering to large corporations. Through being able to demonstrate that it is 'a member of the X organisation' it is able to claim with justification that it has access to additional staff and skills when it needs them. Not only is this a help in the negotiating process, but it gives them the confidence in the first place to bid for, as well as to win, large contracts.

Conversely, we may find our size and public profile a disadvantage. In such cases we might consider asking for negotiations to be held in the strictest confidence, as a prerequisite to talking at all. This stipulation is frequently made where sales and purchases of businesses, or mergers and take-overs are concerned. Indeed, where one of the parties is a listed public company, and where the scale of the talks is large enough to influence the share price, the strictest confidence may be essential.

Let us consider if there are any ways in which our profile might positively assist us in discussions.

Some organisations find that their size can be used psychologically to intimidate the other side, such as by holding discussions only on their own, impressive premises: by fielding the largest conference rooms, the most opulent company cars, by providing extensive dining facilities, by keeping visitors waiting, etc. If such devices do not offend your perceptions of business ethics, nor those of your organisation, be prepared to use them. And be prepared to find the other party using them too, if they apply.

Other organisations simply use their size and/or high reputation as a facilitating factor, realising that the other party will normally prefer to deal with an organisation they know of and can trust.

Sales and marketing profile

The terms 'sales' and 'marketing' are sometimes used as if they were synonymous, so it may be worth defining them. 'Marketing' is the process of defining what people need, and how and where those needs may be satisfied; 'sales' is going out and making sure that they buy.

We need to consider the following:

---

1. Does the negotiation for which we are preparing have general marketing significance to us?

2. Is a successful outcome going to open up opportunities for future sales over and above the immediate subject matter of the negotiation?

3. Do we know what those opportunities are, and how much they might be worth to us?

4. Who in our organisation is concerned in such matters?

5. Are they aware of what we are planning to negotiate, and are they being given a stake in the outcome? (Might they even be members of our negotiating team, perhaps?)

6. What is the immediate sales significance of our proposed deal?

7. Are there quotas or other targets that have to be met, or to which our organisation attaches special significance?

8. Are we sure we know what these are, and their intrinsic value to us?

Financial profile

Because the assumption is often made that 'everyone wants to secure the most and to pay the least', it may be worth devoting special attention to this area. We should ask ourselves whether we are expanding or contracting, or remaining stationary as an organisation.

The significance of this will be to focus attention upon which matters to us most – turnover or profit. It is commonly assumed that profit – 'the bottom line' – is what every organisation is chasing all of the time. More often than not this is true. But consider an insurance agent who can increase the commission rate on all of his business if he reaches a given level of turnover; or a newspaper publisher who can substantially reduce his paper costs per ton if he increases his purchases beyond a certain tonnage of paper per week. Such people are – at least for the time being – more concerned with 'doing the business' than with 'doing profitable business'. Are we aware of our own profile in this respect, and if not, from whom can we find out?

Remember, also, that 'step functions' can work either way: we might be on the threshold of a deal that could increase our costs disproportionately. If this is so, what is the least we dare settle for in terms of profit?

Cash profile

Many businesses are short of cash, even though they are sound financially. This means that for long periods of time they owe their bankers money on overdraft even though they have assets to back such loans. To such companies, the cost of waiting for payment is the current bank base rate plus several percentage points.

If our organisation is in that position, there is value to us in delaying payments for as long as possible and in receiving money as soon as we can, even in the form of returnable deposits, stage payments, and such like. Conversely, if we have a surplus of cash on deposit, the interest we receive on it is likely to be quite insignificant in percentage terms. Therefore, any delay in receiving payment for goods or services will hurt us far less. Indeed we may be able to charge interest on such late payments. If the rate for that interest is even slightly higher than the bank's deposit interest rate, it may actually pay us to do so. If the other party has the opposite cash profile to ours, this will represent an opportunity to negotiate a better deal that will be to both parties' advantage.

Risk profile

At its simplest level risk can be divided into that for which we carry insurance and that for which we don't. If, for instance, we operate a large fleet of goods vehicles under a master policy that covers their contents as well as the vehicles themselves, an offer to supply materials to us c.i.f. (cost, insurance and freight) may be of little value to us if the figure quoted is much in excess of the 'ex works' price.

Conversely, a proposal to us that we execute work on an oil rig at sea may represent a risk that we do not understand, have no claims record for, and for which insurance cover might be both hard to obtain and expensive. It may be in our interest to negotiate in the first case for a tight ex works price. In the second instance we might consider:

(a) quoting only to deliver the materials at the nearest port to the oil rig, for collection by the customer

(b) inviting him to have our insurance included in his master policy, which is often a less expensive insurance and easier to arrange.

As part of the negotiation we then address the issue of how large a price adjustment is to be made in each case.

But risk is not solely concerned with insurance. We should also consider how familiar we are with the nature of the work we shall be negotiating about.

It is always simpler and safer to deal with subjects that we know a good deal about, and which we and our organisation have dealt with before. It is the unknown that brings the greatest hazards. The time to consider such matters is before we meet the other side. If we are negotiating upon familiar ground, we must be sure that we have the right people with the relevant skills available to us at the time when we are going to need them. If we know we are to be on unfamiliar ground, we should be certain we are as fully briefed as possible. If need be, we should consider delaying matters until the necessary expertise is available.

Risk is also concerned with the significance of the forthcoming negotiation within our organisation as a whole. It can be important to know where our operations fall within the scheme of things. Are we expected to produce a given level of profit or other return within a class of business that is not expected to 'rock the boat' organisationally? Or have we been commissioned to open up new fields of endeavour with the inevitable additional risks of failure if things go wrong? In extreme cases it has been known for businesses to undertake known loss-making operations merely to keep afloat until market conditions improve. We certainly need to know if this is the case so that we can plan accordingly. Dire straits can justify high risks.

Technical profile

There may be a technical profile that we need to consider. For example, are we producers of high-quality precision items to precise tolerances? If so, and if our prices reflect this, how does that match up with the other side? Do they come to us for quality regardless of price, or are they merely seeking 'something that will do the job'?

We need to consider the whole area of levels of precision, and examine how closely they match with the needs or capabilities of the other side. A major opportunity for 'trade-offs' may exist between two parties where one is accustomed to a level of quality far in excess of the needs of the other side. A rather more dangerous situation may exist where one party is accustomed to providing a lower level of precision or quality. The difficulty here may arise from the fact that the less precise provider may not appreciate the significance or need for qualities that he is not accustomed to, and may quite unwittingly mislead the other side – both as to his capabilities and as to that party's needs.

The problem is only partly addressed when one side or the other is operating within an internationally recognised quality standard, such as ISO 9000. The problem with such hallmarks is that they frequently address the subject's internal management disciplines rather than the actual specification of the product. The answer sometimes lies in the use of the term 'specification' rather than 'quality'. 'Quality' can be a subjective and judgemental term; 'specification' requires us to state exactly what an item is and is not.

Operational profile

A list of considerations may be useful:

1. What are the internal and practical matters that may affect our fulfilment of any undertaking we may make to outside bodies, or may influence what kinds of service or support we might require from them?

2. If we are a manufacturing organisation, how large is it, and how flexible are our arrangements?

3. Are we in a high-volume flow-line or mass-producing enterprise that requires 'just-in-time' supplies to precise schedules and delivered to stipulated warehouses, goods inwards bays or subject to other disciplines of that kind? In such cases, we shall be constrained by the need to negotiate only with suppliers who can meet those conditions.

4. How large a share of their market do we represent, and to what extent are there alternative sources of supply?

If we are in a sales negotiating situation, we may be governed by the need to find high-volume outlets who will take our products 'straight off the line'. Achieving a successful negotiation in that respect might be as valuable to us as winning the highest price for our goods.

If we are in batch production, or specialise in one-off manufacture, our approach can be more flexible. Less emphasis might be placed upon predictability and smooth flow, and in return we may be able to bargain for a higher unit price when selling. In buying, we may be constrained by uncertainty. The 'rushed job' calling for components that we do not regularly stock can lead us into situations where we are controlled by the market. A negotiation in these circumstances may hinge upon the kind of deal whereby, in return for a guaranteed turnover from us, the supplier is willing to shorten lead times without charging premium rates.

Another internal aspect to be considered is stock or inventory. Many mass-producing organisations have little capacity to hold stock, either of raw materials and components or of finished goods. Such organisations become heavily dependent upon the flow-through associated with just-in-time supplies, partly to contain the amount of their capital employed in the business, but also because they simply do not have the space available. If we are in that situation, we have to remember it when we are bargaining. If, on the other hand, we have stock-holding capacity and the other party does not, there may be opportunities for trade-off in that respect.

Procurement profile

To some organisations, procurement or buying is a routine, low-profile activity conducted by 'anyone who has a budget', hopefully coordinated at the very least by a central unit that controls issue of purchase orders or other supporting contractual documentation. In other organisations it is a highly developed operation with its own manuals of procedure and processes. Indeed negotiating with one's own buyer can be every bit as exacting as selling to a buyer in someone else's firm.

We need to consider where our own operation lies on this spectrum, and how our planned negotiation interacts with our buying function. This can be especially important where we are negotiating to procure items required by a product that is to be sold onward to customers with their own terms of purchase. The buying unit needs to be involved – either in briefing us or in fielding a member of the negotiating team – and made aware of the ultimate terms of supply, which may have to be 'fed down' the chain of procurement. This can be of particular importance in government or defence business, where specialised terms and conditions are applied. Some of these actually require the ultimate customer to have access to all contractors' and sub-contractors' premises. Such terms are usually non-negotiable, and form part of the 'boiler plate' without which negotiation cannot proceed.

Other profiles of significance

At this point, we should pause and reflect upon any other facets of our own organisation that may have an impact on the deal that we are about to do.

1. Do we, for instance, have highly sensitive trade secrets that must be protected at all costs?

2. Is there a formula that may not be revealed to the other side, such that it might impede the normal flow of goods and services?

If, for instance, we market a well-known cola drink, whose secret formulation is crucial to our worldwide market, extra-special precautions may have to be taken in licensing agreements permitting others to bottle our drink. We shall attach additional weight to items such as trade-mark licensing, and the imposition of a duty to help us police the use of the mark. If we are licensing franchises to a brand of snack bars or fast-food chains, special attention will be paid to the 'trade dress' to prevent others from 'passing off' their business as ours by making it appear similar to the casual customer. In such cases we shall need a member of the negotiating team who is familiar with intellectual property rights in our own particular market.

Other matters that may constrain us include official secrets. This is a specialised area, well understood by contractors operating in the defence market. A keynote to much of it is the 'need to know'. In many commercial negotiations one or other of the parties does not have a 'need to know', even though they might find it very convenient to know. The Official Secrets Act, however, is not concerned in the least about this. A breach of security can be a serious breach of statute law. Have we considered all of the implications?

Our company culture

When we come face to face with representatives of another organisation, the more confident we feel about our relationships with our own colleagues, the more able we shall be to demonstrate the confidence that goes with a successful negotiation. Here is a useful checklist:

1. Are we happy that we know and understand how our own organisation operates?

2. Who are the decision-makers?

3. How do we obtain access to them in an acceptable way?

4. How much authority do we have?

5. What are the processes for getting that authority reviewed, extended, or even reduced (for it is not always an advantage in bargaining to be known to have the power)?

Our commercial support

Having reviewed all the internal and lateral aspects of our own entity and how it operates and what its priorities are, let us now turn to the immediate support that we may expect from colleagues who are likely to be close to us and our operation. In some negotiations, executive meets executive to reach decisions in principle, leaving legal or commercial staff to meet later to finalise the details. In other cases, negotiations are conducted in teams that represent all the main functions: sales or procurement, technical, project matters and commercial interests. Whichever approach is taken it can be important that the principles of team negotiating are understood in advance.

Before anyone meets the counter-party, a rehearsal – or at least a team briefing – should have been carried out, unless our team know each other very well and have defined and understood roles or methods. The spokesman for the organisation, if there is to be a single person occupying this role, should know what all the various functional interests are, and what weighting should be placed upon each.

Cultures and styles

It may now be appropriate to consider what is known and understood about the style of the other party.

For instance, do they have a large commercial function, such that every negotiation is a 'team' effort and one seldom meets anybody alone?

It can be important to know this. Some organisations that place a high value upon contract negotiations will seldom receive visitors, or visit another party's location, except as a team of at least two or three – maybe more. If that is the practice, we should be wise to allow for it. Although low priority matters might be dealt with by one of our number, a solo visitor is usually at something of a disadvantage when confronted with a team. The psychological ascendancy is usually with the other party. Team efforts usually produce the better results. Whilst one member of the team is speaking, and our solo member is responding, their people will be observing, thinking ahead, and making notes. When confronted with such a counterparty, we should always try to field at least two people when meeting them. Although it may be better to match their size, strength for strength, almost any number greater than one will help to redress the balance.

Negotiating with organisations of this kind can often appear over-expensive and bureaucratic, but beware. Most of them would not operate in that manner if they did not feel it was to their advantage.

Questions of national culture

Now let us consider some cultural differences that can vary according to ethnic background and the part of the world from which the counterparty comes.

Negotiating in Anglo-Saxon countries

On the whole, British negotiators are most in tune with other Anglo-Saxon races, notably in the United States of America (USA) and possibly Germany and Scandinavia. The pace tends to be brisk and businesslike. Legal or contracts experts may be fielded, and even though there are distinct differences of view, there is a common wish to get the negotiation concluded within a reasonable time, so that everyone can get on with the job.

In the United Kingdom, there is sometimes a degree of 'my word is my bond' dating from the eighteenth-century coffee-house culture within the City of London. This is much less strong than it used to be, now that financial markets are global, and dealers seldom meet at all, let alone in the bars of Throgmorton Street.

In the USA, however, there tends to be a brusquer 'let the buyer beware' mentality. Everyone is presumed to have access to a lawyer. Most people use them extensively in business. The law in the USA is itself less predictable than in the UK, for even though most state systems are based upon common law, the court and judiciary processes are much more diverse and geographically spaced. Everyone is presumed to be 'street-wise'. If people in business get their fingers burnt through not closing legal loopholes, counterparties tend to be less than sympathetic. This is particularly so where overseas entities are trying to break into US markets.

Latin negotiating style

In the Latin countries, not only is the legal system different, but so also is the way of doing business. Much more stress is placed upon forming personal relationships as a basis of trust. This may be done by extending hospitality, but above all by taking the time to do it. The 'quick deal' is much less common and can be fraught with danger. Consequently, he who wants to finish the negotiation by Friday night is likely to end up with a very expensive outcome, the details of which may not have been agreed until late on Friday afternoon. Apart from this being a matter of temperament, there are practical reasons for it as well. In some civil or Roman law countries, the legal system is based much more on the 'letter of the law' than on the parties' intent. Processes can be quite intricate and formal, similar to some of the procedures used in Great Britain by notaries. In routine business matters, suing a counterparty is not such a simple or straightforward matter. Therefore, establishing trust at the outset, and taking time about it, can be a worthwhile investment.

Negotiating in Arab countries

In Arab countries where the legal system is based upon Koranic law and principles people are not in a hurry to fix deals. They will take time. It can be important whom you know, and who knows you. Going to law can be a tortuous business, and best avoided.

Negotiating in Asia

In many parts of Asia the very act of contemplating legal proceedings is regarded as confrontational and unfriendly. One does not take one's company lawyer along to a contract negotiation. That would be taken as an indication that you were expecting to act in a truculent manner, either now or after the deal has been struck. If you feel the need to have a legal specialist present – and if you are wise you probably do – tact demands that you introduce him as 'contracts executive', 'commercial manager', or some similar title.

It is quite common for organisations from Asian nations to field quite large teams of negotiators. Beware of how ostensible authority is used and sometimes concealed. The 'team boss' may not be the person who leads the negotiations and conducts affairs. Sometimes the quiet team member, who says little, takes detailed notes, and apparently speaks little English, is actually the one who carries the rank. He is quietly observing all that goes on, and thinking ahead. It is always wise to treat such people with respect.

Negotiating in the former Soviet Union

Soviet Union negotiators used to have a reputation for carrying no authority whatsoever. It was said that, whoever you spoke to in the Kremlin, only Joseph Stalin had the power to agree to anything. The standard riposte to such situations – 'Take me to the real decision-makers' – was not always felt to be a wise negotiating stance. Matters are very different in Russia today. There are, however, a few lessons to be learnt. In such countries, where medicine is difficult to obtain and expensive, people often have recourse to folk or herbal remedies. One of these is garlic, said to be very effective as a remedy for the common cold. When negotiating in such territories during the winter it can be wise to provide your team with their own supply of garlic cloves, for reasons that will be obvious!

Gifts and hospitality

When doing business with some nationalities, notably the Japanese, the etiquette of giving and receiving gifts needs to be understood and observed.

Typically, such gifts may be quite small, such as a tie-pin bearing one's company logo with suitable variations for any women present. There will be a gift for each member of the opposite team, and something similar will be expected in return. Similar etiquette applies to mutual entertaining, and the Anglo-Saxon attitude of 'I never give or accept gifts or hospitality; that's corruption' can be taken as highly insulting. The use of time in negotiating is also well understood. Woe betide the team that indicates that it has its return flight booked on a particular day.

Marshalling our team

A key task to be undertaken in advance is to marshal the members of our own team, and to ensure that all the relevant and necessary skills are represented. If any are missing, care must be given as to how matters are to be arranged to cover for it. In addition it can be worthwhile to consider the roles that each should play. In some organisations it is the culture for the one who carries the rank internally to drive the negotiation, calling upon others to participate as and when their own speciality is under discussion. As the Japanese well know, there are other ways of doing things.

Most of us negotiate best, and with greatest confidence, when we are talking about a subject we understand well. Consider in advance which subjects are likely to arise, and who are our key specialists in those areas. Candidates to lead the negotiation will include these people.

It is sometimes assumed that there must be a single leader throughout. This is not necessary; in fact, it can be more effective if the leadership is allowed to change from time to time. The important point, however, is that there should be a mutual understanding among our team as to who is going to lead on which subject, and if possible an understood code of signals. These can be agreed in advance and may include:

1. I want to assume the leadership, because I think I have the key knowledge here.

2. I want to pass the leadership to another. This subject is no longer in my field of experience.

3. It's time we ask for a recess to discuss matters between ourselves.

4. This is going badly. We must break off before any more concessions are made.

5. This has gone well. Let us stop without further ado, and 'quit whilst we are ahead'.

Whilst it is always possible to express these signals openly so that the other side is aware of them, there can be times when discretion is useful.

Harnessing personalities

We have already looked at the various ways of measuring personality types. In marshalling a negotiating team it can be useful to know what the various types are, so that their use can be maximised. If a scale such as the Belbin system is used, it can be helpful if each of the team knows the others' orientation, but it is important that the method is properly understood. Most people have a series of predominant Belbin styles, not just a single one. For instance, a Coordinator may also score highly, though less so, as a Shaper or Innovator.

Each member of the team will probably be capable of assuming any one of a number of secondary or understudy roles. Who should lead will therefore be determined not only by personality but by specific mastery of given subject areas. Whilst there may be an overall leader or coordinator – selected perhaps by his or her in-house rank or responsibility – this should not be taken to mean that that person will automatically or overtly direct all operations. There will be given areas of negotiation, such as legal affairs, in which the legally oriented member of the team should dominate and control. Likewise with finance, technical and other specialist areas. The team that understands this, and which has a smooth and rehearsed way of switching roles in mid-negotiation, is likely to command a lead in actual practice. There may be instances where each member, according to inclinations, will fill the role of leader, scribe or analyser, expert, 'ideas' person, hard guy and soft guy.

The other side

Now let us consider the opposite team. We have considered what is known about them in general, cultural terms. Now let us pay attention to what we know, or can ascertain, about the individuals with whom we may expect to meet and treat.

1. Are they complete strangers to us, or have we done business with them before?

2. Are they 'hard' or 'soft' negotiators?

3. What do we know about their techniques?

4. Do they operate as a formal, hierarchical negotiating team, or do they

pass the initiative from one to another, like we might be planning to do?

5. If we have not met them in person before, have other members of our company worked with them? What can be learnt in advance?

6. What may be deduced by applying the same kinds of analysis to them as we have done to ourselves?

7. What are their sales, marketing, technical and financial profiles?

8. When we meet them, to what extent are we dealing only with the people we may see around the table?

9. Who is driving them from behind?

10. What manner of people represent those driving forces, and what are their objectives?

11. How might this influence the negotiation?

Preparing to meet

Next it is necessary to review carefully what are our needs and what we hope to gain from the negotiation. We should have two questions in mind.

1. What are the possible outcomes that might be to our advantage?

2. Where are the areas of obvious common advantage where a 'win' for us is likely to equal a 'win' for them?

It is wise not to hurry this process. In many negotiations it is barely considered at all, so accustomed is everyone to a 'win/lose' contest. It is much better to consult colleagues, use brainstorming techniques, and list all the possibilities.

The 'BATNA'

Before beginning any negotiation we need to be clear about what we consider to be our BATNA (the best alternative to a negotiated agreement). We need to know where we shall go or what we shall do if the negotiation is so unsuccessful that we have little alternative but to break off talks and look elsewhere.

This process should not be hurried. The better our BATNA, the stronger our negotiating position. List all the prospects and consider their implications. We should be clear that we will never settle for a deal less favourable than our perceived BATNA, so it follows that the better our BATNA, the better our deal.

The 'trip wire'

It follows that, having established our BATNA, we need to decide between us what shall be our 'trip wire'.

A trip wire is the point in negotiation where we have to concede to a position not much better than our BATNA. The trip wire should never be as bad as the BATNA point. It should be a position short of the BATNA that causes us sufficient concern to call a halt to the discussions while we think and talk among ourselves: ask for a recess, in effect.

This does presume that we have allowed ourselves facilities – such as a room removed from the discussions – in which we can meet. If no facilities are available then our trip wire may trigger off a request to break off for the day. But it must be known to all the team so that they recognise it when it approaches. Therefore, when the leader – or any other team member – realises the trip-wire point has been reached, he has only to mention it, probably in an oblique manner, for everyone to 'cotton on' and support him.

A trip wire is not the same as reaching deadlock and having to break off talks altogether. It is a position short of that, which still gives everyone an opportunity to find ways of retrieving the situation.

Using our BATNA

Let us pause now and consider how our BATNA may best be used. To begin with, if we have a weak BATNA, such as 'the other party is the sole source of supply' or 'we need the supplies very urgently and do not have too much time to bargain' then if possible we keep it secret. It may become known as discussions proceed, but never from us. Not until a deal is struck with a 'time of the essence' clause do we even hint that we had nowhere else to go.

Conversely, however, if our BATNA is strong, there is nothing to gain by concealing it. Indeed it may save a lot of time. If the other party knows we have many options open to us in addition to dealing with him, it can only act in our favour and induce more favourable concessions.

The other party and their BATNA

Having analysed our own position as fully as possible, let us now turn to our opponents. Although we shall naturally know less about their position, we can still try to gauge the outlook as seen by them.

What is their likely BATNA? What is the best they can do if we fail to negotiate with them? Assuming they play by rules similar to our own, where would we expect their trip wire to lie? If we cannot be certain about any of this, why not hazard three guesses: 'at most', 'at least', and 'likely'?

It is curious how often the 'likely' estimate turns out to be about right. The mere process of thinking about it concentrates our minds.

Common and conflicting goals

Now let us turn to an analysis of goals. We have listed our own goals or objectives.

Which of these goals are common to our perceptions of the other party's goals? Why? Which are neutral, inasmuch as they are not in conflict? List them all, with reasons for our assumptions.

Write down all the conflicts of interest, with an explanation as to why they are conflicting. Stop and ask whether they need to be conflicting, or whether by re-stating them or viewing them in another light, they can become common objectives. For instance, we may have difficulty in supplying at short notice an item that we know they always require in a hurry. To carry high stocks would not be economical for us. But in return for a long-term contract where they offer us forecasts of volume or turnover and a commitment to purchase solely from us for as long as the agreement lasts, it may become possible for us to obtain terms from our own suppliers that would meet the objectives of both sides.

Once again, it pays to take time to consider all these alternatives. This is best done before any meeting starts, but it does not terminate then. Indeed, the most positive discussions can take place when one side or the other has revealed that some forethought has been given to the matter, and that this side is willing to talk or bargain constructively.

The logistics of the negotiation

Possibly the one key question to ask about logistics is 'Where shall the meeting take place?'

It is usually to our advantage to receive negotiating teams at our own premises. Apart from the fact that we know our way around and do not have to travel very far to get there, it can be the precursor to the secondary question: 'Which side shall draft the agreement and/or keep the minutes and/or records of points discussed and agreed?'.

Whilst it may be more costly and inconvenient in staff time to volunteer for all these tasks ourselves, it undoubtedly gives us a negotiating edge. The team that is playing at home often becomes the obvious choice to provide the secretarial support.

Why is this so important? In a short, simple negotiation it may matter very little or not at all. With a large contract to develop an oil terminal, however, or to bid for an outsourcing venture, it is not unknown for teams to meet every working day for several weeks, possibly stretching over a month or two. Sometimes weekend time becomes necessary. A prime difficulty in such cases is keeping track of one's other day-to-day responsibilities, which do not suddenly disappear because of the negotiation. To be operating within one's own office complex can be a valuable trick to have won.

Conversely, if we lose this round and – for a variety of reasons – find ourselves meeting at the other party's location, then quite a lot of thought may need to be given to providing local support. How are we to keep in touch with colleagues at base? What secure or confidential telephone communications will exist 'on location'?

We may be reasonably confident that communications to or from any hotel we are using will not be intercepted. The same might not be true of communications into and out of the counterparty's premises. We may need to ensure that everyone is supplied with digital portable telephones of the kind that cannot be intercepted.

Another requirement that is not always readily appreciated is the practicality of producing a series of scripts or versions of any document under review. One side or other might table the first version of the contract. By midday on the first session, this may be peppered with amendments. By the end of the afternoon we may very easily have reached version three or four. By the end of week one we may be into version twenty. Not only does this demand a fast, accurate word processing service, but it also requires a system whereby track is kept of the various versions, the amendments made, and when, and at least a brief note of what was altered, why, and by agreement with whom. Typically there will be long periods of discussion when not much changes. Then all at once a new version has been tentatively agreed and suddenly each team is held up waiting for the next draft upon which to comment.

We must consider what kind of support we shall need within our own office to handle this kind of service, possibly for several weeks at a time. Even more thought needs to be given to how it might have to be handled at a remote location. If the negotiation is of sufficient importance and value, hiring a local office suite is a solution that should not be overlooked.

We have discussed elsewhere the use of time in exerting bargaining strength over the other side. Demonstrating that we need a quick deal because we are not really prepared for the logistics of negotiating is not going to give us a propitious start.

Operating away from home

Generally speaking a team that is negotiating away from home needs to open with a series of clear-cut requests for local facilities that the other side may supply. This can have two advantages. The first is that we do not arrive and find nowhere to work, nowhere to discuss progress in private, and no means of typing, photocopying, fax or email transmission, keeping in touch with base.

By opening with a list of demands that are reasonable we not only assure our lines of communication but also demonstrate that we are professional in our approach and are prepared. Our justification may be that we are, after all, travelling to their site, and not the other way round. They are at home and have all the facilities they need at their fingertips. The other advantage in opening with these demands stems from an analysis of the other side's response.

Are they cooperative, or is the general attitude 'That's your problem'? If the latter, what does it tell us about our negotiating stance?

Even if we still wish to do business – and that has to be a matter for debate – we may need to pay much closer detail to our BATNA, and possibly set more than one 'trip wire' to cover for the disadvantage under which we have been put.

If the teams are large enough it may be appropriate to plan an introductory session where the leader or a spokesman from each side introduces each team member, indicating their area of knowledge or responsibility, and any restrictions upon their availability. It can, for instance, be needlessly frustrating if one side's lawyer or accountant has to be absent at the one stage in the discussions where law or finance is involved.

It might then be appropriate to indicate some ground rules before detailed discussions begin. These could include opportunities to break for informal or private discussion and procedures for indicating a failure to agree between opposite numbers in each team, in such a way that the leaders can separately assess the significance of each 'sticking point' before it is allowed to get out of hand.

In some circumstances an indication of the length of time discussions are expected to take might be appropriate. There is no harm in this, provided it is remembered that deadlines of that kind must be flexible. The team that arrives with an irrevocable return flight booked is apt to find the other side pushing them hard as that time approaches, knowing that concessions are likely to be won 'so that we do not miss our flight home'. The same applies to negotiations timed to finish 'by the weekend'. Let it be known that you have other business in the district, so that staying on over the weekend is really no hardship at all.

Initial overtures

With any negotiation of size, especially where large teams are concerned, some thought must be given to initial protocol.

Who makes the initial approach to the other side? What subject matter should be covered? Ought there to be an agenda, so that each team knows in principle the items that are to be dealt with?

Time and thought need to be given to this. In some negotiations there may even be a major preliminary negotiation: about what subjects may be negotiated upon and what may not. This is particularly so where matters of public policy are at stake and one team or the other cannot risk being reported as having been in discussions about a subject that they have previously declared to be 'fixed and not negotiable'.

The continuing relationship

As negotiations proceed, personalities reveal themselves and patterns of behaviour become apparent. Some relationships develop and become positive. Others do not. 'Bad guy' ploys may win early concessions but they often do this at the cost of personal relationships, so that the party that conceded first time round realises later what it has done and cannot wait to 'get back at' the individual they perceive as responsible.

Some of this is part of the cut and thrust of bargaining. There are times, however, when antagonisms between different individuals on opposing teams can lead to a vendetta that may needlessly threaten the whole negotiation. Other members of the team, and especially the leader if there is one, must be aware of these situations as they develop. There may come a time in discussion when the warring factions must be separated, even if this means replacing one specialist with another.

To execute such remedies requires a high degree of trust between members of the same negotiating team. In selecting team members it can be important to consider any internal rivalries that may exist, and ask oneself whether these cannot be settled before negotiating starts. Conflict between members of opposite teams is to be expected, though it needs to be controlled and directed. Conflict between members of the same team can be highly damaging to the whole outcome. It is important to be aware of the possibilities and have a plan to deal with them before they become serious.

Closure

So we finally 'get to yes'. It can be vital to perceive when agreement has been reached, something that may not be as obvious as it seems after a set of discussions lasting many days or weeks.

It is often important to seize the opportunity when it arises. Shake on the deal, or whatever form of display seems appropriate, and disperse the teams quickly before someone finds a trivial snag. The danger in doing this is that some final point that has been agreed or conceded in the last moment of discussion is left off the final documentation. This is where those in the team who are known to be 'finishers' should be charged with cleaning up the documentation, making final amendments, checking everything to the last detail and producing a contract or other document for everyone to sign. There should be a deadline fixed for this activity, and a process of reference should any queries arise.

The fixing of a deadline can be especially important. If matters are allowed to drag on, on the basis that agreement has been reached, a project is starting, and we're all too busy to attend to it, there is a danger that matters will never be satisfactorily concluded. They will lie unresolved until a dispute of some sort arises, at which time it may be realised that no one can remember what was finally decided.

The backup team

It may be argued that once a negotiating team has operated together for a while they know the answers to many of these points without needing to be told. This is probably true, though some teams might do better if they were to re-visit the subject. One matter remains to be stated. Whatever the nature of the negotiation, and whether it be at home or away, consideration should be given to providing a good 'back-up team'. In an important negotiation that team should be always at the ready, day or night. An urgent request for some costing figures, or the need to re-estimate something, or for confirmation on some matter, should be all that is necessary to trigger a response. If the request arrives on Friday night and the answer is wanted for Monday morning, it goes without saying that the backup team will work all weekend – and all night if necessary – to provide the response. Holidays are for later.

Having considered strategy, psychological theories and the need for preparation, we are now ready to move on to Part 2, an alphabetical listing of tactics.

PART 2
Tactics

Aggravation

Introduction

Most of the tactics and strategies included in this book seek to provide ways and means of helping the reader to achieve the negotiator's DESIRED RESULT – either by one's own use or by highlighting the tactic so that it can be recognised and defended when used by the other party. However, consideration of poor tactics may also help us to avoid falling into the same trap.

Anger

'He who loses his temper loses the argument' runs an old phrase and there is no doubt that accidentally losing control is unlikely to win many negotiation encounters. Another old phrase runs 'Don't get mad, get even' and this may make far more sense. Yet, oddly enough, many of those who seek to negotiate in the worst climate (e.g. cold callers) seem to disregard the fact that anger is unlikely to win them any friends – still less an order from their target.

Case study: The way to treat a customer?

Whilst writing my part of this book I was subject to at least ten telephone calls from organisations seeking to sell me their products and services. Although some were polite and reasonable and accepted my 'No thanks, I am not interested', the majority virtually demanded an explanation of why I was not interested.

This seems a strange way to try to negotiate for new business. Not only has the target been subjected to an unsolicited and unwanted telephone call (interrupting their workflow) from an unknown organisation but also he is then expected to be subject to a programmed spiel regarding a product or service which he is unlikely to want. Further, if he seeks to interrupt this spiel to state that he is not interested (which would actually benefit the caller by saving his or her time) he is then subjected to a show of anger.

'Could I speak to the person who authorises payment of gas bills?'

'Speaking.'

'We are XYZ organisation and we can save you considerable sums of money off your gas bills.'

'No, thank you. I am not interested.'

(In somewhat aggressive tone) 'Why not?'

'I don't buy from telesales.'

(Getting heated) 'That's ridiculous – we can save you pounds...'

'I have told you I am not...'

(Interrupting) 'But that's silly...'

(Replacing phone) 'Good morning.'

Whilst one accepts that the caller was probably untrained and had simply been given a list of telephone numbers and told to call them to try to gain an interview for a sales representative to call (a scenario which itself is hardly a good advertisement for the organisation), common sense dictates that insulting the recipient of an unwanted call is hardly likely to endear you or your organisation to them. Such callers need to remember that it is unlikely that their target was sitting by the phone with nothing to do other than field their cold calls. Such calls in normal working hours are almost certain to have disturbed attention being given to other work as it did in this case, although providing a classic example of how not to negotiate!

With this in mind a negotiating spiel such as the following might disarm the target and at least lead to them listening to the rest of the presentation.

'Hello, I am sorry to disturb you but we have a product that we thought you might be interested in – it can save you 10% of your annual gas bill. Would you be interested in that sort of saving?'

After all, most people's reaction to the possibility of saving ten per cent off their gas bill would be at least a passing interest. Whetting the appetite in this way should enable the caller to get a figurative 'foot in the door'.

This is reminiscent of Aesop's fable of the contest between the wind and the sun to remove an overcoat from a walker. The wind said that it could use its strength and blow the overcoat away – whereas all that happened was that the walker hugged the coat even more tightly around him. The sun, however, simply gently heated the temperature and swiftly the overcoat was removed – thus proving that persuasion is usually (though not always) better than force.

Keeping cool

To progress negotiation it is essential to keep cool. Losing one's temper may trap you into making threats, many of which are a form of bluff – and recognisable as such. If you bluff you must be prepared to have your bluff called. Keeping cool allows you thinking time and indeed may create pressure on the other side akin to that created by SILENCE.

If provoked to annoyance:

(a) take deep breaths

(b) pause

(c) drop the level and pitch of your voice. Speaking very softly may interrupt the flow of the other side as they strain to hear what you are saying. If the other party then loses their cool, simply keeping quiet may hand you the initiative. If there is no response to angry or intemperate words, the other side is left punching cotton wool – never very satisfying.

Case study: There is such a thing as bad publicity

A company had been featured in the trade press for flouting one of the rules relating to the supply of one of its products. An article highly critical of the company was published and the chairman was determined to respond. He asked the secretary to draft a letter. The secretary refused, stating that the best course of action was to ignore the matter since by the time the next edition of the paper (a weekly) was published the story would have been forgotten. Answering the paper back would, he contended, only provide it with more data, on which a further article could be based.

The chairman insisted that a letter be drafted and sent. As a result, the dispute was given considerable publicity and rumbled on for two months.

In certain cases of course, deliberately losing one's temper can be an effective ploy – see also TEMPER – FALSE and TEMPER – REAL.

Alternative dispute resolution

Introduction

For really serious conflicts, where a negotiated settlement has proved impossible, recourse to alternative disputes resolution (ADR) may be preferable to resorting to legal action which tends to polarise attitudes and lead to an essentially confrontational situation.

The concept

Under ADR both parties agree to use the offices of a mediator to settle their differences. To implement such action it may be necessary to agree on the possibility of such an appointment in the initial stages of a contract, even to agreeing on the name of the mediator to be used. Whether this agreement is reached at that stage or as a result of a dispute, where both parties wish to move to a swiftly resolved settlement, a mediator is jointly appointed and jointly funded, with both parties agreeing to accept the mediator's decision as final. The mediator collects evidence from each side, considers the merits of each party's case and then makes a decision.

It may be helpful to stipulate in the terms under which the mediator will operate that what is required is a decision and/or settlement:

(a) where the terms and requirements are absolutely clear

(b) which covers all the relevant features of the dispute

(c) which is in full and final settlement of the dispute.

The administrative advantages of dispute resolution are:

(a) it may be cheaper than the legal system (see below)

(b) the introduction of a third party should introduce additional objectivity and/or a fresh view of the dispute, possibly even leading to innovative solution(s)

(c) the mediator may defuse antagonism caused between the parties by the dispute and encourage fresh impetus towards a solution

(d) in dealing separately with each party in confidence the mediator may become aware of alternative solutions which neither party wishes to disclose to the other possibly fearing it may weaken their hand.

The advantages over the legal system are:

(a) it should save at least one whole set of legal expenses

(b) there should be savings on legal costs generally

(c) it should save time in considerable argument between the parties

(d) it should lead to an informal resolution of the problem that will not be exposed to public scrutiny

(e) there should be swift resolution rather than potentially interminable delays

(f) it can result in less antagonistic feelings being generated so that a continuation of the relationship, despite what has gone before, is more likely.

A UK Centre for Disputes Resolution was set up in 1991 and in the first eighteen months of its existence dealt with business disputes involving over £550 million. For more information, contact 100 Fetter Lane, London EC4A 1DD, telephone 0171 430 1852. Information is also available from individual courts.

In mid-1996 the Commercial Court issued a practice statement that encouraged judges to invite disputing parties to use ADR procedures, recognising that the process can save fees and time, protect continuing relationships and provide a greater degree of flexibility in originating solutions. Judges making the suggestions are able to assist the parties to choose a suitable person (from a list maintained by the Commercial Court) and to suggest a procedure. The judge then takes no further part in the hearing or action.

Assumptions

Introduction

The problem with assumptions is that a very large proportion turn out to be false. Assuming that the other side will jump a particular way, take a particular course or make a particular suggestion or counter-suggestion may be a dangerous delusion. Set out below are some common assumptions and their inherent dangers – together with suggestions for avoiding the dangers and maximising the effect in your own favour.

1. Bluff

The main problem with bluff is that it can be called. If it is, we may be forced either to backtrack or to take the course of action we stated (even though we did not really wish to do this at all!). However, there is another problem with bluffing, which concerns the perception of the other side regarding the seriousness of the effect of the bluff being called and action being implemented. If the opposition does not have the same perception of the import of the action then our bluff is virtually ineffective.

Case study: So what?

A consultant had carried out work for a client for a number of years but this year the invoice for the work remained unpaid for several weeks despite reminders and telephone calls to the (new) contact. Eventually the consultant faxed a letter stating that unless the invoice was paid within seven days the matter would be referred to his solicitors for recovery. No payment was forthcoming and the solicitors advised notifying the Chief Executive. Within four hours his secretary was on the phone apologising for the non-payment which was purely an oversight.

'But why didn't the threat of solicitors being involved prompt action?'

'The trouble was the person dealing with it this end is new and very junior and had no idea of what that meant – so she simply put the letter on the file with the reminders.'

2. The other side will follow the script

The real trouble here is that the other side may not wish to follow the course that we have plotted for them. Indeed, our proposals may not even be part of the scenario that they have constructed.

Obviously this emanates from a basic lack of understanding of the other side and their requirements from the negotiations.

Case study: Bluff called

A managing director was determined to get some realism into the wage negotiations. When representatives of the trade union asked for what she felt was an untenable and unrealistic wage increase, her reaction was to indicate that in that case the company would need to lose a number of staff.

'Fine,' came the reply. 'We will agree to that – as long as it means that we get the increase we want.'

Believing that the union would not wish to put their members out of work, the managing director assumed that, faced with redundancies, the union would modify their demands. However, their aim was to get to a pay point for the majority regardless of cost and the implications for the minority.

Key technique

As a ploy, the question of 'a rise in return for increased productivity' is sound. Where the MD went wrong was in making a statement rather than posing a question. If she had said 'The only way we can contemplate a rise is by considering redundancies to pay for it, and the greater the rise the larger the number of redundancies. How do you feel about that?', she would have retained control and discovered something of the other side's game plan.

These days she would also need to consult those being made redundant (or their representatives), which might also have given her a lever (generated from those adversely affected) against such an act. Experience indicates that some workforces faced with such a choice opt for a lower pay (or fewer hours) and a preservation of jobs.

---

3. The other side is wrong

Regrettably this assumption is made by many who attempt to deal with customer complaints. Rather than being positive and attempting to see things from the point of view of the disappointed customer, they view the problem as one of defence of the organisation. In many instances their attitude (i.e. that this is a 'try on') may be the case but the assumption that all such calls are 'try ons' is entirely false. This attitude overlooks the fact that it is cheaper to retain an existing customer than to source a new customer. The customer who senses that the organisation is assuming that he is making a false claim is unlikely to repeat his purchase – lose 10% of your customers like that and in less than six years you will not have a business. Customer care and complaint handling should be a matter of converting disappointed customers into satisfied ones, not indicating patent disbelief in their concerns.

4. Convening a meeting will sort it all out

Most negotiations tend to be conducted fairly informally (particularly over the phone) although inevitably a proportion (e.g. those with a high profile, political overtones, and/or which are complex) may need the formality of a meeting to determine detailed points. However, the assumption that placing all the negotiators and their teams in a meeting 'will sort it out' should be challenged. Meetings involve (indeed require) formality and of themselves tend to negate the informal, concession-generated 'deals' that work in so many cases. In addition, the formality of a meeting may create an atmosphere of confrontation – not least if the two sides sit on opposite sides of the table.

A confrontational atmosphere can be aggravated if there are junior personnel (or advisers) present whose secret agenda may be to try to impress their superiors (or principals) and thus create sticking points which a relaxed negotiation – particularly one conducted over a meal – might have averted.

Case study: Sticking point

A solicitor was used to negotiating property matters where the issues revolved round relatively small but important points of detail. In this area his sound advice was usually accepted. A meeting was held to finalise the acquisition of a business and he attended. However he brought the same attention to detail to the meeting and, determined to protect his client, adopted a very aggressive attitude on relatively minor points which threatened the continuation of the discussions. The solicitor's principals requested a recess during which they pointed out that the value of the point he was arguing was £20,000 maximum whereas the deal as a whole was worth £1.5 million and that unless they gave way on the £20,000 the other side could withdraw.

> **Key technique**
>
> In part this was the principals' own fault for not setting out the exact basis on which they wished to conclude the deal, but some of the effect was created by the formality of the meeting, since previous negotiations had been conducted informally by phone and post.

Finally, if negotiators do not require decisions swiftly, each meeting may generate a follow-up meeting, particularly under pressure from those who see the occasion as one that panders to their imagined importance.

5. Relative importance

Because we are sure we understand the relative importance of the negotiations and individual terms to the other side, we can be trapped into believing they have the same perception.

> **Case study: Take care**
>
> A retailer provided a personal service rather than selling normal consumer goods. Therefore, she wished her shop to be open for trade from 10 a.m. until 8 p.m. Monday to Saturday and 11 a.m. until 5 p.m. on Sunday. These trading hours were very different from those in the lease which she was asked to sign. Her solicitor advised her to sign the lease and to sort out such details later, but she refused saying that, if she signed, her freedom to argue had gone – she would already have committed herself to the terms of the lease. Eventually the matter was raised with the landlord who was adamant that he could not allow a change from the normal retailing hours. The retailer walked away from the deal and the lease. She could not have done this had she signed the lease and her business would have been hampered by totally inappropriate restrictions.
>
> > **Key technique**
> >
> > Professional advisers may be excellent at their job but may lack a perception of the practicalities involved. Those who negotiate need to understand the desired result thoroughly.

6. Giving concessions means giving in

There are different views of concessions. Some may see them as a way in which two parties with joint yet differing interests move to a situation where they can both be reasonably content with a deal. However, some people assume that granting a concession (any concession) is a sign of weakness and thus must not be done. Further, if a concession is offered then that must be a sign that the other side's position is weakening and can be exploited. Thus the assumption that pressure can bring further concessions may be rudely shattered and what were reasonable negotiations can become very confrontational.

7. Pressure generates concessions

Aggressive people tend to feel that, because it often does, their aggression can always win them a negotiation. However where aggression meets aggression or even assertiveness, such bullying tactics may not only fail but ensure that the initiators fall back position is also lost.

Case study: Loser loses all

An agency had been retained to supply domestic help to a family on a number of occasions. This time the family had changed its requirements at a late stage and it had proved impossible to find a replacement. The wife had rung to check the position and, when the situation was explained, asked for her money back. This was returned minus the administrative charge levied in accordance with the terms.

The husband then rang to demand repayment of all the fee. It was explained that due to the changes it had proved impossible to supply the domestic help required and that the administrative charge had been deducted in accordance with the terms. The husband became abusive, referred to the 'poor service' given the family in the past and demanded the full fee as a refund in view of the failure to supply. The agency pointed out that his wife had complimented the agency on its service in the past, had changed her requirements at a late stage and the failure to supply was wholly due to this change. In the circumstances there was no way in which the fee should be refunded in full.

The husband continued to be abusive but then changed his attitude and suggested that the agency keep the whole fee and try to supply again. The agency's response was that it was not prepared to work for someone with his attitude – or to send staff to the family since it felt that his attitude was hardly conducive to good treatment.

---

8. Ignorance is bliss

'Ignorance of the law is no excuse' is a very old maxim that many have had cause to rue. Unfortunately, many people ignore the rule and the need to negotiate before agreeing to terms and conditions that could mean that they place themselves in an untenable position when things go wrong. Assuming that the worst cannot or will not occur is foolish. In negotiations it is vital to review the worst case and consider whether it can be lived with – and if not, whether it can be minimised.

Case study: Unnecessary liability

In the past the first tenant of a lease was liable for the payments due if that third party defaulted even if they had sold their interest in the lease to the third party. Until the UK property recession of the early 1990s, this law was neither generally known nor often enforced. However, as tenants were forced out of business, a number of landlords took action against those who had sold their interests but who were still legally liable.

Several tenants who then faced financial penalties had been advised when taking leases to try and negotiate this privity of contract liability out of the lease but refused stating it was unlikely to affect them.

Key technique

The law changed on 1 January 1996 and there are now additional protections for such tenants. However, in negotiating their liability, those who do so without appreciating the full impact of the responsibilities they are acquiring (or assuming that they will not be bothered by their impact) are being extremely short-sighted.

---

9. Price is everything

In some instances it may be, but this is not always so since often there are other important factors that need to be clarified. The situation where one side agrees a price without such details infers an assumption that both parties know what will be included. This is dangerous since, if the price has been shaved to get the job, the items that the purchaser thought were included may be quietly dropped with the reason 'Oh no, of course we didn't include that in the price'.

Case study: Don't fence me in

A client wanted three long fences round his garden replaced. When the job was measured he discussed the requirements – concrete posts and gravel boards, treated panels, new gates, etc. – but was concerned that when the quote arrived, for a little more than he had guessed it would be, there was no detailed specification. Accordingly, rather than discussing it on the phone, as had been suggested by the supplier, he wrote accepting the quote and stated that he understood this to include all the items he had raised at the time of the estimating, including a requirement that he see and approve the style of the replacement gates before they were installed.

> **Key technique**
>
> If this was a ploy by the supplier to leave scope for cutting back on what had already been discussed, it backfired by the simple process of the client supplying the missing specification. Of course, if the supplier did not like that move he would need to respond that 'so and so was not included in the price'. If so, then negotiations are still ongoing – but better that before any work is done than finding the work completed without the items specified and a bill to be paid.

10. Any negotiating indicates weakness

Some parties to agreements seem to feel that to attempt to negotiate indicates that they can't afford the price and that this is a reflection on their financial status. They assume that to gain the respect of the other party they should 'pay up and look big'. This is the height of foolishness, since in many cases there will be an expectation that a certain amount of negotiation will ensue and, since it may be convenient to 'give something away' to get a deal, many sellers will slightly load the price to buy their own concession. Paying the asking price (other than where there is known competition) may be an expensive conceit.

Case study: 'I'll take them – how much are they?'

A company was divesting itself of some trading shops. A manager decided his future lay outside the company and decided to buy some of these shops. He approached the director responsible and asked the price. This was given and included a small mark-up which was expected to be lost during negotiations.

'I have no intention of haggling – I'll pay the price you want.'

'Don't you want to see the shops and their results first?'

'No, let's get on with a deal.'

'I really think it would be against your own interests not to consider the results, to pick the best and not take the lot – they are not all good.'

'No, I'll take the lot at the asking price.'

The director felt that having twice tried to caution the manager he could hardly push it further and concluded the deal. Quite quickly the group of shops began to lose money – partly because of the charge for the money paid to acquire them and partly since some of them were poor sites. Eventually the group went into liquidation.

Key technique:

'Caveat emptor' means 'Let the buyer beware'. Sellers have a great deal going for them in a negotiation – they know the goods, they know the quality, they know the flaws. Buyers have to rely on their (almost inevitably imperfect) assessment of the factors. Paying up to 'look big' involves a massive assumption.

---

11. The other side has read the same negotiating books

The problem is that every negotiation is different. Even if every aspect – price, goods, quality, delivery, etc. is identical in two different negotiating encounters, the scenarios will be completely different simply because the people involved are different. We dare not assume that our opposite number will operate in the way that the textbooks indicate they should – indeed even in a way in which they know they should act!

People are irrational and subject to all kinds of extraneous pressures. We only have to consider the incidence of road rage. Most people are reasonably considerate yet subject them to heat, noise and above all delays on their journey and they can become quite irrational to the point that instead of acknowledging a poor piece of driving on their part with an apologetic handwave, assaults, some serious, even on occasion resulting in death, result. If our opposite number has had such a journey to work, he or she may be less likely to be amenable to our negotiating ploys even though resistance may not be in their interest or that of their organisation.

At times, despite all our wiles, despite our 'knowing' (we think) what the other side wants and despite our 'knowing' (we think) that the deal is good for them, they refuse to bite and the encounter is lost.

Auctioning

Introduction

The oldest trick in the negotiator's book (and his or her sweetest position) is to be simultaneously dealing with two (or more) opposing negotiators (all of whom are interested in either supplying or buying) and thus being able to play one off against the other. Conversely, dealing with a monopoly supplier is totally restrictive.

A level playing field

Where one is in this fortunate position, one has total control. This feeling of control or power can be somewhat overwhelming, particularly as the situation tends to occur rarely and thus be somewhat out of the ordinary run of negotiations. Since one has control, and the other parties lack it, the onus is very much on the person in control to ensure that all interested parties are in fact quoting and re-quoting on the same basis. As in many instances of complex or protracted negotiations, it is also essential to make notes of what has been said to whom so that each negotiating encounter, or step within an encounter, is documented for later reference and to ensure that any changes in the basis for quotation are available to be given to each party on each subsequent contact.

Case study: What's it worth in Worthing?

A decision had been taken to conduct a sale and lease-back arrangement (i.e. one by which the owners of the freehold of a property sell that freehold whilst retaining occupation by granting a lease to themselves) on a shop in a prime position in the south coast town of Worthing. The director was uneasy about marketing the property since he found it extremely difficult to place a value on it, the property being a unique and individual site in a prime position. Accordingly he simply let it be known that offers would be welcomed.

The news swiftly got around and before long there were four interested institutional clients represented by their agents who emerged as serious bidders. Bidding started at around £200,000. This was dismissed out of hand by the director who decided that he preferred to keep control of the whole matter rather than placing it with an agent. Not only did he want first-hand experience of the offers but also he suspected that his organisation would save a substantial fee.

Over the following two months telephone calls came in at regular intervals from the interested parties. On each occasion the director told them the last offer he had received (having added £20,000 to the figure) and noted the new offers being made on a chart with each of the four interested parties listed with details of each conversation. This chart showed at a glance where each party was and what had been said to each.

After eight weeks the bidding had reached £570,000 and the Board decided to call a halt mainly since the rent at that level of capital purchase would be too high for the profitability of the shop.

Rarity

The scenario outlined in the above case study may be somewhat rare and depends for its success on the subject matter itself being rare or unusual – which itself creates a pressure on purchasers to acquire it. When such a situation occurs it should be exploited to the fullest. It may also be helpful to ensure that only one person deals with the various contacts in order to preserve continuity, although even then having two negotiators who can then reply 'I can't see why X should agree to that when we want Y' may further force the bids!

But

Introduction

Most negotiators will prefer to be able to move smoothly through their practised arguments using various tactics, many of which are rehearsed in this book. Although they will prefer not to find that their arguments and spiel are interrupted at each stage, experience may teach them that this tends to occur. When faced with a well-rehearsed spiel, it is essential that the flow is broken. A party faced with such a negotiator may be able to win points by the simple interpolation of sentences beginning with 'But...'

Case study: Butting in

Let's assume an encounter between G a supplier and H a buyer. G enters H's office with a proposal to supply 3,000 widgets at a price of £1 each. Since it seems H is likely to nibble, G begins a spiel on quality, general usage and demand, recent improvements, delivery and so forth.

'But,' says H, 'what would happen if we wanted 1,000?'

G's train of thought is interrupted. He is back to square one and has to rethink and quote a new (probably different and possibly higher) unit price. He may also believe he has been sent a number of semiotic messages by H – that this customer may not really know what he wants, may be short of cash, may be on short-time production (we'll ignore for the moment that these may be entirely false impressions!).

G provides the new quote (let's say £1.10 each) and then resumes his spiel. He tries to deal with delivery matters...

'But,' says H, 'you are talking about a fourteen-day delivery. What happens if we want delivery in seven days?'

G's is back to basics again since a speedier delivery may well have implications on price. He has to think again and requote on the revised basis. (G may also be thinking that H's organisation must be desperate for supplies to try to generate cash.)

He quotes £1.20 each, regroups and mentions quality and how much improved it is.

'But,' says H, 'we don't need such high-grade material – indeed quality of that level is a waste as far as we are concerned. What's your price for less high-quality material?'

G has to assimilate this new environment and, assuming he does not have to check with his own production team first, may be able to requote on the 'second-rate' goods basis. (He may now feel that H is going to move down market to try to pick up some urgent sales.)

He quotes 90p each, and returns to his prepared list of data to mention and comes to the question of finance and deferred date of payment...

'But,' says H, 'we have plenty of cash at the moment and deferred payment is of no value to us at all. What's your price if we pay cash on delivery?'

G is now into a whole new ball game. His interpretations of the 'changed situations' H was putting (or 'butting') to him are entirely wrong!

His original pitch was to sell H 3,000 widgets at £1 each on a deferred terms basis. Now he is apparently down to 1,000 widgets at 90p with immediate payment. Since he has put across deferred terms as an advantage to the purchaser he is now under pressure to give a discount to recognise the value of cash. He quotes 85p and continues by stressing that he needs firm commitment to get the items in within seven days...

'But,' says H, 'suppose we did after all want 3,000 of the second grade quality on seven days but paying cash?'

G may now find it difficult to avoid not quoting less than 85p since an order for 3,000 with swift payment should be that much more valuable than an order for 1,000. If he demurs about going any lower, H might have one last try.

'But,' says H, 'what if I give you a cast-iron confirmed order instantly and you can use our fax to transmit it to your production people this morning?'

G will be under considerable pressure to agree so much so that he may actually put his own organisation under pressure (i.e. negotiate internally on H's behalf!). If this occurs H will have manipulated G into being his ally to get a non-standard order delivered in a non-standard time.

Obviously H would have had to prepare for this encounter – in short to have all his 'But' questions ready. In part, however, what allowed him to move towards his DESIRED RESULT was that by his interposings he was creating conflicting concepts in G's head concerning his (H's) basis for negotiating. G was in fact being conditioned by H to accepting his move towards a low price with a swift delivery. Trying to second-guess what is in the other party's mind is part and parcel of negotiation and if we get it wrong we may well lose the encounter (or at least not win as well as we could).

Concessions

Introduction

Negotiation is a matter of give and take. No tactic illustrates this more effectively than the concept of giving concessions in order to make progress towards a DESIRED RESULT. Effectively, however, it should not be forgotten that with a concession one is actually 'buying' such progress since virtually every concession has a cost. Ideally, no concession should be granted without gaining something in return – a QUID PRO QUO. If this occurs, then buying progress may be quite legitimate. If it does not, then any additional concession is really a bonus – although it could be argued that even a bonus as a closing gift may buy (for example) the goodwill of the other side which could be valuable with an ongoing relationship.

Range of concessions

In MOVING TOWARDS EACH OTHER BY DEGREES, of which the granting of concessions is an extension, some examples of concessions that could be made are listed. Some of these are given below.

(a)   free stock (same product)
(b)   stock (free or at an advantageous price) of another product
(c)   better rate/bonus for quantity
(d)   additional credit
(e)   sale or return instead of committed order
(f)   speedier delivery
(g)   prompt payment
(h)   gifts (personal or organisation-related)
(i)   extension of subscription time
(j)   delaying of price increase.

Trading

Ideally, before beginning any negotiations, the desired result and any BATNA (best alternative to a negotiated agreement) should be listed as should the range of concessions that are available so that these can be used to progress the negotiation.

Case study: Sold

A buyer wanted a car but felt that the price was slightly high. He had a car to trade in and, having hesitated when the dealer offered him a price for it, had pushed up the price offered for it as a trade-in by £150. He really wanted another £100 off the price and suggested to the dealer that he allow the trade in at the previous price plus £100. The dealer replied that he couldn't go to that but he would tax the car for six months (worth about £70) and the deal was done.

In such a situation, the dealer has far more power than the buyer. Unless trade is very slow, there will always be someone else to buy. Only if the buyer can walk away and the dealer wants to move stock will he approach equality of power. The dealer has all the information and the buyer little.

Conversely, if the buyer knows that there is a similar model in another dealer's showroom just down the road – and is prepared to walk away to that dealer – he could use that information to gain another concession, by telling the dealer of the other model. This might win a further concession. Indeed, in the terms of the deal being considered above, another £50 might make all the difference. The buyer will feel he has won and the dealer has gained a sale – the classic WIN:WIN situation.

Precedents

The problem with giving concessions is that they can become a precedent. If so, then far from becoming an aid to the successful outcome of a negotiation, they can become a hindrance since the party that won a concession previously may tend to expect one on each occasion.

Case study: Insolvent

A debtor had been chased for several months by a trader and it was obvious that he was in serious financial difficulty. Eventually the trader offered to write off around 25% of the amount due in exchange for immediate cash settlement of the rest, but that this concession would only be effective if the cheque was in his hands within 48 hours and was met at first presentation. This was agreed and the transaction completed satisfactorily.

Some years later, the debtor started taking unauthorised extended credit once again and this time the trader chased for payment far more promptly. The debtor offered a cheque for 75% of the amount outstanding but this

---

time the trader refused and threatened legal action unless payment was forthcoming. The debtor was incredulous. His reaction was the result of his belief that once again the '75% for instant payment' would bring agreement.

This is the danger of such concessions. Indeed it is possible that, the second time around, the debtor had actually costed his purchases at the 75% level believing he could repeat the concession.

> *Note:* *One is tempted to wonder why the trader did not provide pro-forma invoices the second time around so that payment was made at or before the time of trade. Indeed with a new or unknown client this itself is a valuable negotiating device, allowing the concession of credit or 'account customer' to be granted when one is satisfied regarding credit-worthiness – a factor that can be referred to in the TERMS.*

'He is well paid who is well satisfied'

So said Shakespeare and the quotation should remind us that satisfying the other party may involve many matters other than payment – even including some that we ourselves do not rate at all. But our estimation of value is not important. What matters is the other party's estimation. There are many constituent facts of the average deal:

(a) time of delivery
(b) manner of delivery
(c) quality
(d) add-ons
(e) confidence in performance
(f) the concession previously listed.

Sometimes these peripheral 'add-ons' may assume an importance larger than other factors in the mind of the other side. Indeed, meeting (or even better exceeding) the other party's non-financial constituents (which we perceive – or are told – to have what we may regard as a disproportionate importance) can be used to work to our advantage if we are mainly preoccupied with price. Indeed, in a time when mistakes and errors seem widespread, the fact that we can meet requests, that we achieve deadlines, maintain quality and so forth, and that we are known to do so may enable us to command a premium price for the goods or services we offer. Not having to chase for delivery, to return faulty goods, to pester for satisfaction and so on, saves time, conflict and aggravation.

Finding the key

We need to spend time trying to discern what it is that the other side really values highest among the constituent parts of their side of the negotiations. There is little point in asking the direct question but talking round the subject may well assist – as of course will an appreciation of what has gone before. Chatting to the receptionist, the person conducting you to the office, to the secretary, may enable a picture to be formed of what is required.

'The despatch bay seems very congested' – 'Yes we've got a lot of orders waiting for widgets' is a harmless little exchange but tells the widget salesman that speedy delivery may be essential. If the company opens the meeting with the comment that 'Our MD's prime requirement is to provide speedy delivery', this may strike a chord with the buyer. Whilst cost cannot be totally ignored, the thought of being able to convert non-productive stocks waiting for parts into finished goods very swiftly could be very attractive to the buyer – not just for the company but also for the buyer personally. He may be very satisfied with an instant delivery even though the price may by slightly above what was originally contemplated.

WARNING: It should not be overlooked that the information in the exchange could be MISINFORMATION. The supplier might have been deliberately taken through the stock room in order to plant in his mind the need for quick delivery. If his mind is concentrating on meeting that requirement, it may overlook the fact that the buyer is trying for a keener price!) Being able to think quickly and to react to changed circumstances is essential.

BATNA

If negotiations and concessions and incentives all fail we have the situation where we must break off talks with the other party – if we can. If we can't, then we may have to accept the best we can get from the other party so the breaking off may need to be on the basis of 'I need to take further instructions'.

Debt-chasing

Introduction

Debt-chasing is probably the area of business where negotiation is needed so much that it is almost a matter of routine. The problem is that so often the only excuse for lack of payment is lack of intent, and this can lead the unwary negotiator into a situation where AGGRAVATION is endemic.

Very often the odds are stacked against the creditor. He may have already supplied goods and services that are now under the control of the debtor – as is any move towards issuing a cheque.

This may be a situation in which anger is entirely justified, but is it likely that anger will achieve the desired result? Assuming polite reminders have gone unanswered, it may be hardly surprising if irritation seeps into the encounter. Unfortunately however, anger tends to generate anger which can lead to a loss of control. During that loss of control things may be said which would have been better left unsaid. However, the speaker may now be committed to what has gone before – backtracking, even if the sense of the alternative can be seen, involves losing face and many faced with such an alternative will prefer to battle on.

An alternative?

In such a situation right may be on the side of the creditor – a fact that even the debtor may accept even though it may not be admitted. If anger will not work, covering every eventuality may be the answer.

Checklist

1. Compile a file of the situation commencing with the order, name and authority of person placing it, date and specification, special requirements, etc.

2. Obtain the delivery note or similar evidence that the goods or services were received by the debtor.

3. Ensure the invoice was correct in every detail – addressee, date, amount (including extensions), reference, etc.

   Note: *Most invoices indicate terms of payment; few indicate what will occur if such terms are not met. It may be worth considering adding to 'Terms: Total due 30 days from date of invoice' wording such as 'Interest at 2% above base rate will be added to amounts not paid on time.' It may be argued that such a requirement is too late a notification and that it might be helpful to refer to it in the terms of the contract.*

4. Detail previous attempts made to chase payment including what has been said. If points have been raised by the debtor (whether genuine or not), set out the answers to such points, indicating, where the point is not considered to be genuine.

   Note: *Unless all points are covered the debtor may still have a chance to delay whilst the point is addressed.*

5. Contact

(a) With the foregoing the creditor has complete control of the information relating to the matter and this can be placed before the debtor. If further points are then raised by the debtor the answer again is to address them calmly and to make a note of them. If they have no validity, then this can be added to the résumé.

(b) If payment is still refused the point may need to be made that there seems to be no alternative to taking legal action for recovery – stated not with anger but as a fact and with regret. In addition, it should be made clear that all charges incurred will also be sought from the debtor. Again it may be advisable to insert this proviso in the terms since for claims being made under the Small Claims arrangement (i.e. for amounts up to £3,000) solicitor's costs are not normally reclaimable.

(c) Rather than instituting legal action immediately it may be helpful to allow a further 3/6 days for payment to be made. This not only shows further reasonableness but also provides some means of saving face. However, it should be made clear that there will be no further direct contact (i.e. no further chances of discussion and delay).

(d) If payment is not received then the file of data already prepared will form the evidence that will be required by solicitors before they commence action. With such information, action can be taken swiftly.

(e) Throughout, the attitude of the creditor should be one of cool regret rather than heated threat.

Note: *Experience indicates that very often some of the data will not be available due to inefficient or faulty procedures (or poor application of sound procedures). If this is so then the case will be weakened since the 'audit trail' is broken. There is little that can be done in this instance, but it is important that gaps and breaks are rectified to make the situation even more 'cast-iron' next time around.*

Legal moves

For some years the matter of late payment – which is a peculiarly British practice – has been the subject of attention by both the United Kingdom Government and the European Community Commission. Whilst it seems unlikely that there can be workable legislation on the matter, the essential problem remains one of commercial reality: 'Do I want this person's business knowing that I will be paid late, or do I do without such business?'

Several ideas for improving what is basically a habit and a means by which an organisation can operate in an under-capitalised state have been such put forward. These ideas include:

(a) statutory interest on late payment (there is nothing to stop creditors charging interest on late payment, although obtaining payment of such interest may cause further problems)

(b) stating payment policies in documents of record (e.g. annual reports)

(c) outlining statistical evidence of payment periods (although such statistics, since they are calculated at a year end can be easily manipulated).

Since prevention is better than cure, it may be advisable to prepare our business assuming that there will be instances where debtors will try to avoid paying us due amounts. The following steps should be considered:

(a) ensure terms are updated, clear and brought to the attention of those with whom we deal so that the 'I didn't know' ploy cannot be used

(b) supply on a small scale only until a payment record is established and from which no deviation is allowed

(c) maintain strict credit control – immediate and constant chasing once the due date has arrived and the invoice is unpaid – is carried out and full details of every contact and every statement is made

(d) establish strict procedures and the fact that what is said will happen does happen, which may gain us a reputation for strictness over financial matters

(e) immediately stop supply of goods once there is a problem with payment

(f) resume supplies of goods after a stoppage only via pro forma invoices.

Levels of authority

It should not be overlooked that non-payment may be other than deliberate. This could be because:

(a) the invoice has been mislaid (so supply a copy)

(b) the person to whom it was addressed has left and the invoice is buried in unregarded papers (so discover who is now responsible and supply a copy)

(c) the person to whom it was addressed does not wish to pass it through the system as it will (for example) have an adverse effect on their budget.

This may mean that the person concerned did not have authority to place the order in the first place. The lesson from this situation is to ensure – tactfully – that the person placing an order has the requisite authority. This might be incorporated in the terms along the lines of: 'This order is being fulfilled on the understanding that the person placing the order has the requisite authority. In the event that this is not so, the purchasing company by its acceptance of these goods/services confirms its liability for the purchase and undertakes to pay in accordance with terms or the goods must be returned undamaged and in their original format.'

Where non-payment is due to the invoice being blocked, it may be necessary to go over the head of the person concerned and to recite the history of the invoice to a senior manager or director. Again, having all the information available is essential so that the history can be rehearsed. If legal action has been threatened this can be referred to as very often senior personnel may be more aware of the potential public relations damage that such an action could cause. The danger of course is that it is unlikely to endear the supplier to the original contact and thus this form of negotiation may be best used only when the invoice relates to a one-off service or supply.

Desired result

Introduction

The purpose and aim of negotiation is to try to convert another party (or other parties) to one's own view or way of thinking, often with financial implications for both parties. Although this may be difficult where both parties are principals and able to 'deal' on their own account, it can be even more difficult where they are negotiating on behalf of a principal whose views are not their own personal preference yet they have to 'toe the organisation line'. Regardless of the circumstances, all too often those who set out to attempt a successful negotiation end up with their aim defeated. Often the reason for this failure to achieve what was required is that somewhere along the way their own ultimate aim or 'desired result' was forgotten.

Define it

'It' in this context refers to the desired result. Before undertaking any negotiation, a prime aim of the negotiator must be to determine exactly what it is that (s)he wishes to achieve. This may not be an absolute since, although there may be an understandable wish to 'achieve as much as possible whilst giving away as little as possible', most negotiators must know that achieving their best result may be unlikely and they may have to concede points as per the 'MOVING TOWARDS EACH OTHER BY DEGREES' concept. However, at all times, they need to keep their ultimate aim in the forefront of their mind's eye (or even on a pad if negotiating on the phone).

Maintain it

The problem is that often, particularly should negotiations become heated and/or involved, the negotiator can become sidetracked and may lose sight of the desired result. Maintaining the movement towards the result is essential even though sidetracking may be unavoidable.

Case study: Blanking out

A supplier felt that it was vital that a better unit price was received for the product being sold and telephoned her customer. After the usual pleasantries, and before the supplier had a chance to raise the question of price, the customer remarked: 'I'm glad you phoned. We have a problem with quality of your product last month. Have you got production problems?'

Immediately the supplier's desired result – increasing price – has been blanked out by an immediate problem – real or imagined. There is no question of dealing with the price increase before the quality question is resolved.

'I'm extremely concerned to hear that. I'll send our quality control people over immediately to check the position. I must say it is very unusual with that product...'

If the supplier ended the sentence at that point there is an opportunity for the customer to respond negatively. However, she went on: '...particularly as we have recently improved its composition at considerable expense...'

This has now turned the conversation (albeit somewhat one-sidedly) back to the question of costs: '...which is why I was ringing you. Obviously we will sort out any quality problems and replace any product that is substandard. However, our concern at the moment is that the more expensive components we are now including have eroded our margins and we see no alternative to adjusting our prices.'

'It seems illogical to talk of adjusting prices when the quality is suspect,' retorted the customer.

'Not really since, as I just explained, your quality problem is very much a one-off and we have already promised to investigate and rectify that. Here I am talking about future supplies. We do have some leeway in terms of time and in view of your present problems I am prepared to defer the new prices for three months. That's a concession purely to your organisation and I am sure it will be agreeable to you.'

Whether it was agreeable or not, the point is that, despite being nearly derailed immediately, the supplier has nudged the discussion back to her desired result – increasing the prices – and by giving a 'concession' implied that the customer is 'getting a deal'.

Achieve it

In the above case study the supplier achieved her desired result mainly because she could both think quickly and respond positively to the possible derailment of the conversation. This cannot be done without adequate preparation and thus an inevitable concomitant of the desired result is the ability to consider all the arguments that could be thrown at one by the other side – and, of course, not just think of these arguments but also sort out some satisfactory responses to them. It is an important point to avoid being fazed by responses. Whilst it may be good tactics to gain time by responding 'I'll have to think about that and come back to you' (which may well be more advisable than trying to think on one's feet whilst unprepared), it does not necessarily demonstrate good control and, in any event, means the desired result has been lost – at least for the length of that encounter.

Other results

Of course, in the encounter outlined in the above case study, it could be argued that the supplier had an underlying and possibly longer-term desired result – that of retaining the customer as a repeat customer – in which case, depending how strong was her need to retain the customer, she may need to condition her pressure to satisfy her immediate desired result to avoid imperiling her longer-term result.

Settling for second best

We will not always achieve our desired result since often the interests of the two negotiators may be diametrically opposed. For example, in rent review negotiations very often the aim of the landlord is to obtain as much as possible in terms of an increase in rent, whereas the aim of the tenant is to keep any increase to the minimum. During their negotiations they will usually each concede some movement and find a compromise with which they can both live.

(Actually in such a situation the landlord's desired result is not strictly as stated above (i.e. to obtain as much as possible...) since the rent is only of value to him whilst it is being paid. If the rent is pitched too highly so that the tenant cannot afford it and goes out of business, the highest rent in the world suddenly loses much of its value. Continuity and consistency of payment may be just as valuable as the amount. It is for this reason that tenants with good reputations as payers can sometimes achieve a reduced rent that takes account of this valuable fact.)

Disguises

Introduction

It is estimated that in over 60% of negotiation encounters success can be achieved if from the outset the party initiating the encounter sets out to ensure either that the other party

(a) does not lose face

(b) is seen to have had some impact on the encounter

(c) can be said to have 'done a good job'.

One definition of a good negotiator may be someone who can manipulate his or her opponent in a way that at worst there is a neutral result and at best the result is that both parties seem to win.

Winning

Referring to SARAH, we see that the H stands for Handle the subject matter with appreciation of the feelings of the other party. If we can make it seem that the other party has won as much as we have won, everyone will be satisfied except that in our case it will be a double satisfaction since we alone will know that we achieved our outcome in accordance with our own plan. The simplest form of such a negotiation is set out in the following case study although the ploy has become so widespread that it may not work as well in the future as more and more recognise the manipulation.

Case study: Price-fixing

A manufacturer wanted to move the price for one of his products from £2.20 to £2.50. He realised that suggesting an increase in price well in excess of 10 per cent when RPI (retail price index) inflation was less than 4% would be regarded as excessive although he could prove the product inflation of some of his own raw materials was running at twice the RPI figure. He decided to telephone his largest customer to give him advance warning of the price increase so that he would have a chance to buy in against the increase at the current price. In addition, he wanted to be able to conclude what was bound to be a difficulty encounter by leaving the customer still feeling as though he had done a good job and feeling reasonably well-disposed to the supplier.

Accordingly when he broached the subject of the price increase he made it even steeper than necessary: 'I'm afraid we've got to move to £2.60 a widget.'

'£2.60! But that's an increase of 18% – inflation's only around 3.5% at present,' said his customer, thinking 'Hell and we've run our stocks of his product right down to improve cash flow.'

Key technique

Having a calculator next to the phone is a good device so that one can instantly calculate increases, the effect on one's margin and so forth and throw the statistics back as an instant rebuff.

'Yes, but you will recall we haven't increased our prices for over two years so we have a great deal of catching up to do.'

'That's all very well but we're all suffering from margins being squeezed as a result of lower demand levels following the recession.'

'You don't need to tell me. Unless we can reinstate our margins we can't see any way forward. That's why we thought we would not put the new price into effect until 1 January so you will have time to put two or three orders in at the old price.'

'Well, that's something I suppose,' mused his customer, thinking that at least he could rectify his low stock position at the existing price and would also not have to re-cost the price of the goods including those forming part of a big overseas order where there was currently very little profit, 'but it's still an 18 per cent increase and there's no way we can pass that on to our customers.'

'How much do you think your market will wear?'

'About 8 per cent at most.'

'Mmm, tell you what. We obviously don't want to lose your business and would like to help. There is no way we can only increase by 8 per cent but what we could do is to delay the price increase for you on firm orders placed up to the end of January rather than the first, and use a price of £2.50 thereafter. But that's a special deal only for you and I would want your undertaking that you would not divulge the price you are paying. I can't go any further than that.'

Faced with this kind of solution most customers tend to accept the deal. They can claim that by their efforts at negotiation they have reduced the price increase by 25% (if they really want it to sound good they could claim they have reduced the increase by 33% of the increase imposed!) and also gained another month's purchases at the existing price, which, if they have funds available then can exploit by overstocking at the old price.

Stop

The last sentence of the manufacturer's conversation is an indication to the buyer 'Don't push me'. By hearing the words 'I can't go any further' the buyer realises that he may be near the end of the negotiating road and without any further ammunition to support his views he will lose if he tries to push for more. Since no-one likes losing there is a message/advice to leave matters where they are now – having 'won' a reduction in the original increase and the deferment of the implementation date.

See also SARAH.

Disinformation

Introduction

The key to successful negotiation is information – see Getting Our Act Together in Part 1. The more information one has – particularly about the tactics, attitudes and range of options of the other side – the more likely one is to be able to succeed in one's endeavours. If we can also gain an insight into the reactions of the other side by providing information, apparently unwittingly, this too can be a valuable ploy. The information that is either deliberately or accidentally leaked is usually genuine and tends to be for the purpose of testing resolve or reaction. However, entirely false information can also be leaked or made available – and again the purpose is to condition the opposition.

Creating a false awareness

Whilst somewhat devious there are a number of well-recorded instances where letters or figures containing false information have been left lying around apparently accidentally, with the intent that a target should read them. Believing themselves to have 'discovered' information preferred by the other side to be kept confidential, their own actions and attitudes have then been conditioned by the information provided. Often the belief that they have been 'clever' to have discovered such information may obscure a true and objective analysis of the situation. They will also be unwittingly put in the position that they will 'know' something that the other side does not want them to know, but in fact the other side will know the whole situation and will know that their reactions will be conditioned by the information that they have had 'planted' on them.

Case study: The false price

A director owned a car which she wanted to sell. She knew her secretary's fiancé needed a car. She asked the secretary to type a letter to a local auction entering the car with a reserve of £17,500. She was out of the office that afternoon and telephoned her secretary to tell her to leave her letters on her desk and she would sign and post them herself. When she returned she destroyed the letter to the auction house as she felt she was unlikely to get more than £16,500 for the car.

The following day the secretary said that she noted the director wanted to sell her car and her fiancé was prepared to offer her £17,250 for it. The offer was accepted and the deal done.

The letter switch

Similar disinformation can be communicated by switching letters to a third party with one to an adviser so that the third party receives a letter to an adviser 'by mistake' and thus has information which he believes the other party does not know he has. The scope for planting such information is considerable – although it should not be assumed that the third party will always accept the information as genuine.

Embarrassment

Introduction

Negotiators tend to operate best when free from any restraining influences and worst when constrained by factors that restrict their freedom of action. Nowhere is this more the case than when an impasse in negotiations could become public knowledge with a knock-on effect on the reputation of the business itself. Inevitably this consideration restricts the freedom of action of one party – and enables its exploitation by the other.

Case study: No insurance against bad publicity

A company was obliged under the lease to refund to the landlord the cost of insurance of the premises they were leasing from the landlord. One year the premium sought to be recovered was charged at £16,500 which was thought to be excessive.

The tenants, convinced that they could get a better deal, obtained an alternative quote at £6,600 through their own insurance brokers. With written confirmation of the alternative quote, which evidenced that the same material facts had been used to obtain it, the tenants sought the landlord's permission to substitute their own cover for his. This was refused.

'In that case,' said the tenants, 'we refuse to pay more than £6,600 for the insurance premium, since that is the price given us by the market.'

'You are required under the lease to refund the cost of my insuring the premises,' replied the landlord.

'But this is manifestly an overcharge and we cannot accept it.'

The argument dragged on for several months and eventually the landlord lost patience and threatened to send in bailiffs to the premises to seize goods to the value of the amount demanded.

The landlord knew that the tenants had a high profile – both in the area and nationally – and thought it unlikely that the company would wish the dispute to be made public. The tenants were horrified at the thought, despite their conviction that they were in the right, of it being known that bailiffs had been to their premises and seized goods in payment of a 'debt'. They suspected (probably quite rightly) that few people learning of the event would bother to check the background and would immediately assume that the company was having cashflow difficulties. In turn this would cause a loss of confidence in the company and its products, a potential downturn in sales and a consequent real cashflow problem.

Accordingly a cheque for £6,600 was immediately delivered to the landlord with the request that they be able to approach the insurers direct to discover why they were charging over £10,000 more than the alternative insurers. This was agreed and eventually the landlord's insurers reduced their premium.

Key technique

The problem here was not just the potentially disastrous publicity that could result from the story becoming public but the fact that under property law an insurance premium is regarded as 'insurance rent' and can be 'distrained' (that is a landlord does not need to obtain an order from a court, where it could have been challenged by the tenants, before instructing bailiffs to recover goods of equivalent value).

Reputation, and any potential damage to reputation, places a considerable pressure on negotiators which can slant or even impede their desired result. In the above case the original desired result was 'avoid overpaying the insurance premium' but in reality the desired result was 'minimise any overpayment but not to the extent where our name (and thus financial probity) can be impaired'. The determination of the actual desired result is important particularly where embarrassment could be an important factor.

Compliance authorities use this device in their dealings with organisations with a public profile. If, for example, an organisation is believed to have sold fireworks to a child under the age of sixteen, the Trading Standards officer may advise the trader that should he plead guilty he will receive a warning which will then form part of an official record (to be used in the event of a further 'offence') whereas he may win the case if he can appear in court . However, the danger of a court appearance is the potential adverse publicity – win or lose.

Fingertip facts

Introduction

The best negotiators may be those gifted (or well-trained) persons who can recall immediately a range of facts that will be of assistance to them at the time they require those facts. It is relatively easy to generate data from research but this ability is of little value if it is not available before the event. Being able to quote data at the time in the negotiations when it is of most moment may assist the progress towards the DESIRED RESULT and at least will demonstrate that the negotiator has a professional approach to the task in hand.

For those of us not blessed with such instant recall other aids must substitute.

Distant negotiation

When negotiating by telephone, fax or e-mail, there is little difficulty in having a checklist of data by the device being used to communicate. Indeed by arranging one's office and files suitably such information may be instantly available without the need to prepare a derived list.

Case study: Instant response required

The manager based in the UK was subject to regular requests for information and input from the parent company in the USA. He quickly learned that replying 'I'll get back to you' reflected poorly as this response was often used as a means of avoiding the issue. On the basis of 'If you cannot lick 'em, join 'em', he re-arranged his office so that all his files were behind his desk in a semi-circle. Individual data was loaded on to a desktop PC which was always ready for access. He could now access all his current files by moving his wheeled chair and without putting down the telephone handset and within seconds could have the data on which he was being quizzed on the desk in front of him.

The danger of using the telephone (unless fully prepared) is that there is an inference that speed is essential. The replies to everything one says can be received at the speed of sound without any guidance as to the manner in which they are said – the body language that we rely on for a substantial part of the meaning of every message is absent. Some telephone dealers exploit both the speed and the distance aspects, offering a 'quick deal whilst I have you on the phone, but I must have an instant decision'. The response 'Sorry, I'm in a meeting. I can't consider this now. Give me a ring at [time]' negates the pressure and buys time for the call recipient to consider the offer with the benefit of some research.

Face to face

With face-to-face negotiation the use of files or computer-loaded information is not necessarily ruled out. Indeed with notebook computers a range of information can be stored and referred to whilst the other party is speaking. Even commenting 'Excuse me for a moment, I have some information here about that' hardly breaks the flow of the interaction since it still demonstrates that the negotiator has prepared for the encounter. If this is impossible a simple crib may suffice. This could be clipped to the top of the file or (paper) notebook to act as an aide-memoire.

Having information available in the above ways can not only provide valuable data for the use of the negotiator in his or her contentions but also allows the probing of data put forward by the opposition.

Case study: Fingertip facts

A director was concerned that back-up commentary on proposals to commit scarce capital to projects seemed to be somewhat economical with the truth. Accordingly he prepared a résumé of the financial data shown by old proposals alongside the actual figures derived from the first three years trading of such units.

The next time commentary referred to 'above budget achievements' of such previous projects he was able to quote facts rather than contentions and thus win the negotiating confrontation, and incidentally, improve the return on the capital available.

Note: *This kind of instant information access is of assistance in a variety of situations.* One Stop Property, *a companion volume to this book, includes a property register that can be derived from summarising information data from leases, etc. Having such information presented in an instant access format is invaluable not only when asked for such details but also in negotiations with landlords and agents regarding rent on review, renewals and in respect of new units. Information is power and a lack of information hands the initiative to the other side. In that context being able to quote instantly the percentage rise of rent on the last few reviews and the increase in (say) RPI over a similar period may demonstrate that unreasonable demands are pointless. This will not necessarily win the negotiation but at least it may help focus attention on realities.*

Reliable information

Of course, the information being generated must be entirely reliable. If information is unreliable the situation will be worse than having no information at all.

Case study: Unfortunate briefing

At the Group of Seven summit meeting in Tokyo in July 1993, the USA provided guidance kits to its delegates. Unfortunately the research was somewhat faulty and included the following errors:

(a) the Italian president, who has no executive power and does not attend such meetings, was shown as leading the delegation whereas the Italian prime minister, who has such power and leads Italy's delegation to the meetings, was not listed

(b) details of the other two main members of the Italian delegation, the treasury and foreign ministers, were also omitted but details of the finance minister, who was not due to and did not attend the meeting, were included.

Moral

If information is produced to assist negotiations, no matter what the arena, it must be accurate. If not it may be preferable to forget the idea, as faulty information can lose respect, create communication bars and may even be insulting, albeit unwittingly, thus resulting in the creation of the opposite effect to that intended or required.

Force majeure

Seldom do negotiators actually encounter each other on even terms. Very often one or other will be conditioned by outside circumstances that restrict their scope of operation. Normally skilled negotiators will wish to keep the fact that they do not have a wide scope for negotiation confidential from their opponent although at times the fact itself can be used as an argument. Conversely, knowing that one's opponent's hands are tied can be a valuable piece of information to the other side. Once again, information provides power.

Referral to higher authority

Most negotiators operate at their best when they have a free hand. However, at times it can be very valuable, particularly if progress is not being made, to be able to say: 'Well, I note your position and I have told you mine. I have now gone as far as my brief allows me. Unless you can agree on the terms I have just suggested I will have to refer to [my boss, the director, the Board, the executive committee, etc.] to discover what they want to do now.'

If it is thought that one last push could gain agreement it might be worth adding 'I am not at all sure how they will take it. I suspect they will want me to try a different [source, outlet, supplier, agent, etc.].' The aim of course is to imply that it is 'make your mind up time' for the other side. Unless there is agreement now, then not only is there no agreement but also the dialogue itself may be abandoned.

Like all bluffs (if used as a bluff) the user must be ready to have the bluff called. If the answer is still 'no' he or she must be prepared to walk away – although they could try the HAVING THE LAST WORD tactic as a final attempt!

Finally, it is a device which is probably only capable of being used once per negotiation and it will be worth recording its use on the file.

Denial

Sometimes people are forced to try to negotiate without any real scope for them to exercise any real authority. This places them in an invidious position particularly where this is known to the other side. This is a situation waiting to be exploited.

Case study: Marriage value nets a million

An organisation leased a factory from the Commission for the New Towns. It was fairly common knowledge that the Commission had been ordered by the Government to divest itself of its property holdings. The director realised that with his company sitting on a very long lease at a relatively small rent, the investment potential of the property was low to most outsiders but had a considerable potential to the organisation itself.

When the Commission wrote asking if the organisation was interested in acquiring the freehold and, if so, to name their price, his reply was fairly non committal indicating that the Board was not sure that it wanted to tie money up in land and buildings. He added that since he was obliged under standing instructions to put the matter to the Board he needed some indication of the figure it would require. Knowing the Commission was under orders to divest and that it was unlikely there could be any others interested he felt he could afford to be hard-nosed.

The Commission came back with a figure and after a little haggling it was agreed that the freehold could be purchased for around £75,000 and the acquisition was completed a few weeks later.

This gave the organisation both freehold and their own leasehold occupation. Putting the two together generates a marriage value of the interests. The value in this case, following transferring production to another factory, and offering the whole site for sale with vacant possession, was £1,150,000. A gross profit of just over £1 million netted the organisation in excess of £600,000 after paying relocation and redundancy – about twelve times what the factory was making a year.

Forcing a deal

Introduction

One way of trying to gain the agreement of the other party to an encounter is by using rhetorical questions – questions that more closely resemble statements which are designed to prompt the other side to give an answer already determined by the questioner. This device seeks to gain agreement where it seemed unlikely that this would be the case, albeit the target party may not like the 'agreement' so forced.

Triple-staging

Such rhetorical questioning can be carried a stage further by a persistent negotiator whereby he embarks on a process of three structured phases and, in the following example, telephone calls. Of course, the respondent may not realise until the completion of the last call that he has been manipulated by the caller. Such callers completed their planning and thinking previously and part of the process requires that the respondent does not have time, and does not gain time by asking to break the process and stall the movement towards the caller's desired result.

In this sequence, the caller first raises a question indicating his preparedness to find a suitable and reasonable solution, even if it is not his own desired result. After a reasonable response or compromise has been indicated (forced) at that stage, in phase two the attitude of the caller hardens with inference of threats that could be activated if the desired result is not agreed. Finally, the caller moves to the pre-determined third stage where a deal is suggested.

Case study: 1. Carrot, 2. Stick, 3. Deal

1. Carrot

A director who had been dismissed for incompetency rang a former colleague at his old company.

'How are sales?'

'Not too good but that's inevitable following the recession.'

'I did say you needed to keep sales buoyant, didn't I?'

'You did.'

'Of course, the situation won't be helped by the fact that you've lost some of my contacts, will it?'

'No.'

'Tell you what, for old times' sake, I could speak to a few of my old contacts and get them to place orders. That will help, won't it?'

'It will.'

'Tell you what I'll do for you then – I'll make a few phone calls to my old contacts and tell them that there are no differences between us and they would be doing themselves a favour by placing their orders as before. That's in everyone's interests, isn't it?'

'Yes, I suppose it is.'

(Whether the company colleague thinks this or not he can hardly comment otherwise although he will probably realise that this means the ex-director has an edge.)

2. Stick

One or two days after this conversation, the former director telephones again.

'I've just been with my solicitor and he says that there is a cast-iron case against the company for unfair dismissal, and I should take action immediately, simply in order to protect my position, though that's not in anyone's interest, is it?'

'Not really – I thought we had agreed a compromise.'

'So did I, but he feels that to protect my interests I should take action immediately for the maximum claimable. Obviously the compensation awarded could hit the company hard when things are tough, but since I am paying him for his advice, I have to listen to what he says, don't I?'

'I suppose you do.'

(Once again the rhetorical question generates the answer that the ex-director wants. In addition he has not mentioned the question of the additional sales, which, despite the source, would still be welcome.)

3. Deal

Again a couple of days are left before the ex-director calls again.

'I've spoken to some of my contacts and I am sure that I can put together a number of orders that will help the order book now and cashflow next month. That will help, won't it?'

'Oh great.'

'I've also had another chat with my solicitor who is adamant that there is a strong case.'

'Oh yes.'

'Mind you, it seems a bit pointless for us to argue in a tribunal when we could make the company profitable with my contacts, doesn't it?'

'I suppose so.'

'What did cross my mind was for me to drop the action.'

'That would be good news.'

'Yes, it would save aggro all round. Mind you, I think I should get something out of it. I'd suggest in return you appoint me on a consultancy basis for, say, six months, to try to generate some sales during the present slump. If you pay me on commission it won't even cost you a thing.'

> Note: *This third call contains the 'crunch' and, given the way the first two calls were dealt with, with the initiative retained by the ex-director, it may be difficult for his former colleague to find suitable words to extricate himself and his organisation.*

It can be difficult to recognise the ploy at the first or even second stage. However, the way to negate the intention is to break into the cycle by not agreeing with the rhetorical question and refuting the statements made – or alternatively using questions of one's own.

For example, at the end of the first stage, the company contact could say 'That's an attractive proposition but all contacts are best placed through the company sales force, as you said when you were here, didn't you?' Not only does this bounce the question back to the questioner but it gives the company contact a moment to think. Gaining thinking time is all-important to negate such manipulation – see THINKING TIME.

Gaining the initiative

Introduction

Information is the key to negotiating – information about the other party, their attitudes, prices, concerns, information about timings, quality, quantities, information about how we are going to manoeuvre the encounter so that we can achieve our desired result. Starting negotiations without information (see Getting Our Act Together) is akin to an army commencing battle without adequate supplies of bullets and shells – it may start confidently but without the back-up all will soon be lost. Ideally, we need not just information about the subject matter, our TERMS, any dispute, etc., but also about our 'opponent'.

Who am I up against?

The word 'opponent' was used deliberately above, since that may well be an accurate description in confrontational negotiations. However in many negotiational encounters, both sides may have a shared interest in reaching a mutually acceptable compromise, in which case 'opponent' is a somewhat emotive description. Its use may lead to attitudes and language that are inappropriate and may hinder our progress to our desired result. Regarding the other party as a 'partner' in a joint aim to achieve a result may aid such movement.

Data survey

Regardless of whether the encounter is a move between partners to find a mutually acceptable solution or a confrontational dispute, we still need as much information as possible. The answers to questions such as those appearing in the following checklist may assist. Certainly any assumptions about the other party – experience indicating that the vast majority of assumptions are false – may well hamper our successful negotiations.

Running through a checklist such as the following may focus our mind on their salient characteristics and provide a plan of action.

Information search

1. Subject

(a) Who am I calling?

(b) What is he/she like?

(c) How do they like to be treated?

(d) Can I use their first name to try to make the contact more friendly?

(e) Do I know anything about their personal life that I can use to aid rapport?

(f) Do I know their business background?

(g) Have I dealt with them before and if so is there anything that can be derived from that encounter?

2. Relationship

(a) What is the history of the relationship?

(b) Have there been problems before?

(c) What general/specific information would it be useful to have available?

(d) If the person is unknown to me, what can we find out about them, their organisation, products, etc?

(e) If they are unknown, is there any way I can form a link with them (mutual interest, acquaintance, etc.) or use a third party as an introduction?

   Note: Using a named third party as an introduction may at least obtain a hearing, which could be denied if the approach is completely 'cold'.

3. Timing

(a) Is this a good time to contact them? Telephoning or calling early on a Monday – or the day after a Bank Holiday – or on the first day a respondent is back from holiday is probably unwise. A better response may be obtained after lunch on that day or on the following days. Immediately stating that one hadn't phoned or called the previous day 'because I knew you'd be pretty snowed under' might also create a better rapport than would otherwise be the case.

(b) Has the respondent just returned from holiday and will he be harassed and unlikely to wish to discuss the matter – particularly if it is complex or lengthy?

If the other party is known and the negotiation is likely to be lengthy and/or complex it may be better to write or fax a résumé first so that the recipient does not have to come to the matter cold. Giving information in advance in this way, should improve their retention of the data.

(c) If I catch this person just as they are going home am I likely to get a quick and favourable decision agreement, or are they likely to resent the intrusion into 'off-duty' time?

(d) Would it be better to wait to make contact until they have received some news/data/etc. which shows us/me in a good light and they are thus likely to be receptive to my ideas and suggestions for resolution of the subject matter?

4. Purpose

(a) What do I want to achieve from this contact?

(b) Is the person likely to give me what I want to achieve?

(c) If so, do I need to tread carefully? Will they want something in return? If so, do I want to give this? If not, how do I get out of it?

(d) If not, is there something I can offer that might change their outlook?

(e) Do I have anything to offer to attain the gain?

5. Recourse

(a) Do I need information/a favour from this person?

(b) If so, what is it (list what is required)?

(c) Would it be better to ask for the information in advance so I can prepare for the encounter?

(d) Is there information from our side that it would be helpful to give to them prior to the call to try to gain agreement and/or understanding?

(e) Is there any CONCESSION I can offer that will balance the favour being asked?

6. Dispute

(a) What are the facts?

Note: Often 'facts' are actually found to be opinions or even misinformation. It is essential to find solid facts on which to base an argument. Negotiation encounters built on unreliable or incorrect facts are almost certain to fail unless the negotiator is an excellent bluffer or can think very quickly.

(b) Are we in the wrong (check the facts – see above – and the TERMS)?

(c) Who was at fault?

(d) Do we need to apologise?

(e) Is our position defensible? If so, how is it best defended without being aggressive? If not, what's the worst case and how do we avoid it?

(f) Should we have foreseen what happened?

(g) What sort of recompense is needed? Does the loss concern time, inconvenience, or expense?

(h) Does this have potential effects elsewhere?

(i) Does it have a public relations dimension?

(j) What precedent(s) could this create?

(k) What is my scope/authority?

(l) What is the other party's scope/authority?

(m) Do I have power to deal and/or negotiate?

(n) Am I prepared to deal and finalise this matter here and now?

(o) Would I prefer time to think?

(p) Are there legal ramifications and if so do I need advice?

(q) Do I have any clinchers, trump cards, unexpected items to use to gain my desired result if things do not go well?

7. Administration

(a) What happens if they are not there? Is the matter urgent?

(b) Should I compose a message in readiness to be left – or would I prefer not to alert them to what I want to raise?

(c) Would I prefer to alert them to the subject matter because this may alert their concern and pave the way for my negotiations later?

(d) Do I want them to contact me (in which case this will be at their initiative) or would I prefer to maintain the initiative by making the contact?

8. Follow-up

(a) At end of an encounter, recap what has been agreed, what has been left without agreement, and who is going to do what. Suggest writing notes of the result so that there is a record rather than relying on memory.

(b) What have I to do?

(c) When must I do it by?

(d What have they agreed to do?

(e) When must they do it by?

9. Sundries

(a) Did I listen to what was said?

(b) Did I hear anything further?

(c) Did my attitude change during discussion and if so why?

(d) Should I make notes regarding any of this so that I have a record the next time we have a negotiation encounter?

> *Note:* *With negotiations that are likely to be ongoing, the answer to (d) is almost certainly 'Yes', since in that way we build a data bank of information on the person and subject matter.*

Know thine enemy

This neat phrase is not meant in this context to label parties to an encounter as enemies but to reinforce the need in all encounters for both parties to discover as much as possible about the other. After all, not all negotiation encounters are between representatives of organisations – sometime we are representing no-one but ourself. For example, in applying for a job or for promotion we place ourselves in a negotiating situation: we, the applicant, are selling ourself. As such we should wish to present ourself and our capabilities in a way that will appeal to the interviewer. It should be automatic that we prepare an application form, a covering letter, possibly a very full résumé of our whole career to amplify the content of the application form and so on. This should enable the interviewer to have a reasonably detailed word picture of us before ever we meet and, even though they might be well advised to keep an open mind, to have formed some initial views of us and our application.

From the advertisement or job specification held by the agency, we may have gained some impressions of the prospective employer.

If, however, we carry out some research on the employer, obtain a copy of their annual report, press cuttings, product catalogue and so on, we will be in a position of some strength at the interview – the traditional bias towards the interviewer will have been redressed to a large extent by our knowledge of the organisation.

Not only should we be able to understand more of what is said, but also we can ask intelligent questions related to the information we have already obtained. This has two benefits – the interview will be more meaningful to both parties, and, more importantly to our application, the interviewer should appreciate that this candidate has not simply put in an application but has taken the time, showed some initiative, and researched the company. This could reflect well on us, particularly where the employer is looking for someone with initiative, a self-starter etc.

Case study: Who am I dealing with and where?

A consultant was approached by both phone and letter to present a proposal for in-house training. There was little that was difficult about the project and less that was original – he had dealt with the subject matter previously in a number of locations. However, rather than replying in writing, he arranged to visit the enquirer and to deliver the written proposal personally. Before making his call he researched the company and discovered that it had recently been taken over and restructured.

On arrival he went to reception and stated his business. The receptionist was somewhat offhand with him and after 15 minutes had to be reminded that he was still waiting to see the contact at his prearranged time. During those minutes the consultant was able to listen to one side of the conversations being handled by the receptionist who, amongst others, was fielding calls from complaining customers. The manner in which these calls were dealt with left a great deal to be desired.

Eventually the consultant was shown to the conference room, which was reached by passing several noticeboards. 'Your noticeboards are very full,' he commented to his guide.

'Are they? I never look at them, you can't see anything.'

He went in to the meeting with the benefit of some immediate impressions of the organisation that would not have been gained by simply writing and sending a proposal. His subject? 'Internal and external communications including customer care.'

During the short discussion with the contact, he was able to refer to the takeover and the fact that this must have been unsettling to everyone, leading to poor morale. In making a short presentation, he was able to slant his proposal in a somewhat different way than he originally intended to cover the points he had learned.

Postscript: During the negotiations regarding the acceptance of the proposal, the consultant made the point that he thought it was important to get the 'feel' of the organisation before framing such training and to meet the client. The contact commented that he had asked several organisations to quote but had given the job to the only person who bothered to call and discuss it.

Disarming the enemy

Knowing that the other party has certain arguments that are likely to be used does not mean we should simply prepare defences to the arguments. If we use the facts first we may be able to negate their value. This is a method beloved of media interviewers. If they are trying to focus on an error or misjudgment yet know that the interviewee has some good news with which their otherwise penetrating enquiry can be blunted, they grab the initiative and mention it first: 'Now Mr Barber, I know you are going to say that your environmental record for the last sixty years has been exemplary but the fact remains that this pollution of the River Twirl is extremely damaging to everyone and worrying to you.'

With one sentence the interviewer has removed the effectiveness of Mr Barber's inevitable response to the current problem, stated that the event is damaging and also inferred that the company is worried.

Mr Barber's already prepared comment, 'I must stress that in sixty years of industrial production this is the first time my organisation has ever been involved in a pollution problem' now sounds somewhat tame. In response he might do better to try and regain the initiative in turn and state, 'I'm glad you mentioned our excellent conservation and protection of the environment record as we must all make sure that we don't let our emotions get things out of perspective'.

As well as stressing the record Mr Barber has now inferred in turn that it is the interviewer who is getting things out of perspective. Obviously this is a dangerous ploy and could only be used where the event is relatively minor. Trying to belittle something which is serious merely hands the initiative back to the interviewer.

Good guy, bad guy

Introduction

Although somewhat corny since it has been used in countless films, particularly involving interrogations of prisoners, either in war or police investigation scenarios, there is still evidence that setting up the negotiation encounter so that the opposition has to deal with two types of person – one awkward, aggressive and confrontational and the other approachable, reasonable and flexible – can aid negotiations to a successful conclusion.

Psychological theory

The theory behind this set-up is that most people will prefer to deal with the approachable, reasonable, flexible 'good guy' and if they can engineer a way in which negotiations can take place with that person they will feel that they have 'won' and will not notice that the deal they conclude with the 'good guy' may be no better (or only marginally better) for them than that which would have been obtained from the 'bad guy'. The antagonism with the 'bad guy' creates a clash, leaving the 'good guy' to create a rapport with the third party, allowing both, at least in theory, to manipulate him.

Research in the USA in the early 1990s indicated that 94 per cent of people want to 'get along with' other people. Only 6 per cent were prepared to be difficult to get what they want. Even though 6 per cent of the population of the UK still generates around 3,500,000 potential 'bad guys' the fact remains that most of us feel we can 'do better' when negotiating with someone who is reasonable, who sees our point of view and can listen to our arguments. We may find this 'constructive approach' to our negotiating efforts more satisfying than the tactics adopted by the bad guy so that the effect may be a kind of satisfaction – as Shakespeare noted: 'He is well paid who is well satisfied.'

If the other side has set up the encounter so that good and bad guy are acting in tandem, the other party can be manipulated to their desired result – preferably without them realising it. What is needed is to create an impression that the two negotiators are themselves at loggerheads so that there can be a rapport between one and the other party if only the other negotiator would leave the scene. Normally the 'bad guy' will be the more senior person so that the other party gains the impression that by dealing with the more junior, a deal may be done 'behind the back' of the senior. The 'good guy' suggests 'Let's work together to make a deal and leave it to me to bring [the 'bad guy'] round.'

Case study: Sold at a premium

A company was divesting itself of the major part of its retailing chain and had a number of interested parties. Initially the Chairman and another director dealt with the enquiries on a face-to-face basis. The Chairman was an aggressive individual who more or less told all the potential buyers the price that was wanted and indicated that it was virtually on a 'take it or leave it' basis and that before any deals were done the company wished to check the financial probity of the purchaser.

One potential purchaser (P) was used to concluding deals on a very informal basis – even a handshake. The director knew he had a reputation for never backtracking on a deal even though nothing might exist on paper. This wasn't good enough for the Chairman who wanted a signature on a 'letter of intent'. So much did the Chairman press the point for this signature that the director realised that P might walk away from the deal. Since P was one of the best prospects for a speedy deal, he prevailed on the Chairman to let him handle the detailed negotiations with P, leaving the Chairman to oversee the final agreement.

The Chairman's view was that he didn't like P much and he was quite prepared to let the director continue the negotiations. Swift progress was made by P and the director who even managed to obtain a better rate for the purchase of stock in the shops so relieved was P not to be dealing with the Chairman.

During the concluding part of the negotiations, the director dropped the hint (which may have helped him gain the extra concession on the stock) that if he (the director) got a good deal for this tranche of shops the Chairman might delegate the responsibility for future sales to him. Since P was in the market to build a chain, and he was building a relationship with the director that could bode well for possible further sales in the future, a further additional deal 'sweetener' was obtained.

Having the last word (or 'doorknobbing')

Introduction

Negotiation between those who know each other well tends to require different approaches, although many of the principles set out in this book will still apply. Some tactics may be recognisable as such by those who know each other. In such a situation the target of the tactic may well think to herself 'Ah, I recognise the so-and-so tactic there. I won't let on but will simply use the so-and-so defence.'

However, informal negotiations may require far more careful handling than those between (for example) supplier and customer where after the negotiations have been included, the parties may not see each other for some time. If there is an ongoing relationship (for example, that between employer and employee), there may be a greater need in many instances for the resolution of the encounter to be amicable.

Taking one's leave

Often where such a negotiating encounter has occurred, whether arising informally out of non-negotiation business, or even formally, the more junior person may wish to make a final point. The purpose of this may be either to 'even the score' should the encounter not have gone the way they preferred, or to leave an unresolved point that may enable them to reopen the discussion at a later date, or to indicate fresh facts that may act as a lever to reopen the discussion just 'resolved', or simply to leave the other with a desired impression. Since this kind of point is often made as the person is leaving the room it can be accurately described as 'doorknobbing'! The person using the tactic may be trying to reopen negotiations without it seeming obvious that that is the intent. The impression being sought is the concept of 'I know we have agreed the solution to that negotiation and I must go but I've just been struck by this thought...'; whilst the intent is 'I want to reopen our negotiations either now or some time in the future and here's a thought to be going on with in the meantime'.

Effect

If the negotiation encounter has not gone entirely or at all in the speaker's favour, keeping a 'last word' or 'doorknob' comment that is favourable to the person mentioning it can have the effect of prompting second thoughts about the agreement just reached. Since the speaker will have gone after making the comment, the thought is left 'hanging in the air'.

Case study: Gaining a handle

A manager had asked to see the director to seek a review of her pay. The director had referred to the poor financial results and expressed the hope that an upturn in trade would soon lead to a position where salaries could be reviewed but that at the current time there was simply no spare cash to fund such an increase.

Despite negotiations, that had been the decision. Although the encounter had been assertive and robust, each could apparently see the other's arguments and the relationship was still amicable.

As the manager made to leave the room she turned and said 'Oh, by the way, I meant to tell you that I managed to get the x department to complete that work which we thought we might have to put out to tender.'

'That is good news,' came the reply (what else could he say?).

'Yes, if we can do it accurately, and I am sure from the initial tests that we can, we will save the organisation around £8,000.'

> #### Key technique
>
> Although the 'doorknob' fact might have been used as a valuable part of the negotiation just concluded, the manager held the information back and wants to use it as she leaves the room. The effect is that the 'doorknobbing' comment will be the one that the director remembers.

Second phase

'I was thinking again about our conversation last week and although I do appreciate that there is nothing in the budget, given that I have managed to save the organisation £X by arranging for the work we were putting out to tender to be done internally, I wondered whether you had any thoughts about using part of the budget that is now surplus?'

The negotiation is now reopened when the director thought it was completely finished – and may now be on the spot in terms of seeking a reply.

Defence?

The principle of the 'doorknob' tactic is to leave the way open to restart negotiations. The person subjected to the tactic should recognise it for what it is and make plans accordingly. Whilst there may be a temptation to agree that perhaps they had better review the question of rise in salary, so that the encounter can be closed completely, this should be resisted. It may be preferable to:

(a)   think about it

(b)   check that the facts claimed are in fact the case (after all people often do exaggerate)

(c)   consider whether there is real need and scope for some reaction.

If there is perceived to be a need for some further discussion, then it may be preferable to seize the initiative and invite the person back, rather than wait for them to raise the matter. In this way the director will regain some of the initiative – the discussion will be at his preferred time.

Keeping one's powder dry

Introduction

The injunction to the settlers of the Wild West was to 'keep a weather eye open and your powder dry'. Since they were in a hostile environment they needed to be on the alert and unless their firing powder was dry their guns would be useless to defend them. Similar advice may be given to the negotiator with the additional suggestion of not necessarily using all the bullets to defend the first onslaught. In the PRE-EMPTIVE STRIKE, it is recommended that we parade all the evidence demonstrating an overwhelming argument in favour of acceptance. Conversely, using only part of the ammunition may lead the opposition to disclose their case. Having encouraged them to exhaust all their ammunition, the *coup de grâce* can be applied using the item that has been held back.

Case study: Just a moment

After inspecting furniture in a showroom, a customer ordered some identical to that on display but stipulated that he had no wish to have the showroom model, which had a flaw – and as a result was being offered at a discount – evidenced by a sale label. The salesman assured him that his requirements would be ordered from the factory and some time later the items were delivered. The customer found the item had the flaw pointed out in the shop.

'You have delivered this furniture.'

'That's right, sir – the goods as you ordered.'

'Could you check the order for me?'

'Yes, sir. I have it here.'

'My copy says the goods must be ex-factory.'

'So does mine, sir, and that's what we have delivered.'

'Then why has the item an identical flaw to that which I saw on the model in your showroom?'

'I really can't explain that, sir. We will have to check.'

'I'll tell you what has happened – you have not ordered it from the factory at all.'

'Oh, I assure you we have, sir – direct to you.'

'I tell you you have not.'

'I think you will find that we have.'

'Then how do you explain that the item I have, not only has the flaw I pointed out in your showroom but also has your sale label stapled to the item?'

The salesman was led into either lying or making statements concerning a matter of which he was ignorant. By not mentioning the sale ticket until after assurances of a direct delivery the customer trapped him in the lie. In addition, the salesman knows that the customer knows he lied – not a very auspicious start to the next round of negotiations – resolution of the problem where the customer will now have added ammunition.

Case study: Damaged reputation as well as goods

An upmarket store delivered (late) an expensive video unit. Because the householder was in a hurry to get out, having been kept waiting by the delivery, the unit had to be left in its packaging unchecked. On inspecting the goods it was obvious to the householder that there was damage to the top which presumably occurred in the warehouse before delivery. She called for a replacement and the store's quality controller visited.

'I can see it is damaged but it looks recent.'

'I don't think that is so. You will see the wood is pressed in, whereas had there been damage immediately adjacent to the wood it would have splintered.'

'It's possible but I can't see how we can be liable.'

'Perhaps this may convince you '(presenting the original wrapping material which not only showed a dent matching the damaged wood but also had dirt ingrained within the damaged packaging material).

Memory failure

Introduction

Good negotiators tend to have and to need good memories – or at least good back-up (see FINGERTIP FACTS). Meeting someone who apparently has a bad memory indicates that one possibly can gain an edge since:

(a)   their command of the facts of the negotiations may be faulty

(b)   the fact that they have a poor memory should place us in an advantageous position as they may be a less-effective negotiator.

An effective ploy?

One needs to beware the person with the apparent bad memory as this can be used as a ploy to extend negotiations and keep raising issues once thought to be settled – or to deliberately reopen negotiations by means of a 'false' memory recall. The device is possibly less likely to be effective in the instant one-to-one encounter since the opportunity to 'forget' what has been decided is reduced. However, in negotiations that are protracted or occur over or on several different occasions, one side may be able to refer back and apparently deliberately misunderstand or recall incorrectly what has gone before. The effect may be to wear down the opponent since it can be extremely irritating to be required to reopen discussions on matters thought to be already settled and agreed.

Case study: Now where were we?

On day 3 of negotiations, T recaps what has gone before: 'We agreed that we would supply one generator by 1 September next year and a second by the following 31 March, with payment for both due in full by 31 December of year 2.'

S, interrupting 'Just a moment. I thought we had agreed that payment for each generator would fall due in the December, twelve months after the year of delivery.'

T is now in a quandary since this is at odds with his own recall of the situation but nothing exists that can demonstrate that at least in principle they had agreed the payment timetable to which S had just referred.

'I don't think we did agree that length of credit.'

S: 'Well, that's what I have reported back to my Board. Does it cause you a problem?'

The ball is back in T's court regarding something that he thought was cut and dried. The pressure on him now is to concede a payment date somewhere between the two dates – his original date and S's suggested date from her 'memory'.

Key technique:

A way round this would have been to have noted in writing what had been agreed previously. Even though such a note may not be binding, it would at least evidence what had been agreed in principle 'so far'. This is important where negotiations are broken off to resume at a later date – 'Let's just note down where we are currently at.' If a copy of the note is given to the other side it will become very difficult for them to argue that they didn't know at a later date.

There is a further problem in that even if a note is made at the time the other party can still challenge it as a true record. The answer here may be to record what was agreed between the parties and to give each a copy (noting this fact in the record itself).

Moving towards each other by degrees (or 'salami slicing')

Introduction

Inevitably when two sides to a negotiation start some distance apart and move towards each other, their original positions are left behind. Normally these positions cannot be recovered, although in the case of rent reviews used as the case study here, this may not always be so. The principle in moving from the original position is akin to cutting slices from a salami sausage, concerning which it is said that the best way to taste the sausage is to eat thin slices repeatedly. With movement towards a commonly acceptable compromise, 'thin' concessions may be equally advisable.

Reviewing the situation

Let us take the example of rent review negotiations where the landlord starts wanting £100,000 rent from the date of the next review. The tenant is currently paying £60,000 and feels the maximum justified increase should be around £15,000. They are, on the face of it, a long way apart. However, the landlord does not expect to achieve £100,000 and thinks he might be able to get £90,000 (he also knows that it is highly probable that the tenant will also know this).

However, if the landlord starts at £90,000 he immediately puts his best price under pressure so he adds a bit that he is prepared to lose. (He also knows that it may be good psychologically for the tenant to feel she has 'saved' something even if the saving is actually illusory.)

The first thing the parties need to do is to measure the property. Whenever two people measure a property, the size will differ. Since size will help determine the rent, the tenant immediately has an opportunity to start 'slicing away the salami' by arguing about the area. The smaller she can make the premises appear, the less rent it will command. So every small non-usable area needs to be measured and excluded.

As a result of the measure, it may be that the landlord's £100,000 has to be shaved to (say) £96,000. The tenant may find that her £60,000 is obviously light and that her first offer should be around £72,000. The gap between them has been reduced by two small slices to £24,000.

Using evidence

The next stage is for each side to gather evidence of rents being paid by others in the neighbourhood. Inevitably, the landlord will quote only those rents that show his calculations to be nearer his perception of the 'true value' and the tenant will quote only those rents that assist her. In the process they may have to cut off and add on respectively further 'slices' of rent. The landlord may come down to £90,000,the tenant may move up to £76,000. The effect of two more slices is to reduce the gap to £14,000 from the original £40,000. The difficulty is that the landlord is now at the level he thought was achievable and the tenant is already showing a 26% increase on her rental outgoings and at a level higher than she thought she wished to concede.

From now on, the slices are likely to be much thinner.

(Of course, reviewing the evidence does not necessarily mean accepting what the other party states – all statements need to be checked out so that any bluff is called.)

The next stage

If the tenant then puts forward good additional arguments – the fact that there is an empty property next door, the fact that she is only allowed to use the premises for her trade whereas others have no such restrictions, the fact that she always pays her rent on time and maintains the property in accordance with the lease – it may create additional pressure on the landlord to concede some further slices, perhaps moving him to £86,000 whilst moving herself to £80,000.

Third-party referral

Now comes the tricky bit. Having rehearsed all the arguments and moved some way from their original positions, both parties may feel that they have reached the end of the road in terms of concessions. Normally leases will require the situation to be referred to a third party appointed to determine the settlement.

Additional dimensions now enter the negotiations since:

(a) the appointment of a third party must be paid for by the parties, usually, but not always, equally

(b) although there may be a temptation for the third party to 'split the difference', and for the parties to believe this is what will happen, this is not always the case.

Hence the negotiating control moves away from the parties. The decision on whether to take this step or not requires them to balance the likelihood of gaining a favourable decision against the costs of the action.

Horse-trading

The threat of third-party referral is itself a negotiating ploy particularly where the two parties are only, as here, £6,000 apart.

If they go to third party they will tend to revert to previous offers, say of £90,000 and £70,000 respectively. The fee of the third party (usually 5% of the average of the two opening offers) could be £4,000 plus costs, and so each party would have to think they would almost certainly have to pay £2,500. This would probably be an acceptable cost for the landlord since the new rent is payable for (normally) five years but it is still a bit of a gamble and he might feel he would prefer to give a little bit more in the hope of gaining agreement from the tenant to avoid the costs (and time commitment) of a third-party referral.

The final offer (and the final slice off the salami) could therefore be £84,000 to avoid a third-party referral. To the tenant this might be attractive as she will have to pay between £2,500 and £4,000 in fees and third-party costs anyway, and she has no real guarantee that the rent decided for them might not be more than £84,000. Indeed if it is anything more than £80,000 she will bear double costs in the first year in any event – the third-party costs plus the rent in excess of his previous offer.

> *Notes: In all negotiations such as these which can become considerably protracted it is essential to keep notes of exactly what was agreed and why and when (and not agreed and why and when). Inevitably, there is a certain amount of 'truth economy' involved in such negotiations. Whereas there is little problem remembering the truth, it can be very difficult to remember what lies we used. It is therefore essential that we make notes so that we do not get caught out in our own deception. Once a person gets caught in a lie it can damage their own case – including evidence and aspects not affected directly by the lie. Similar warnings apply to exaggerations.*
>
> *Unless one wants to use a PRE-EMPTIVE STRIKE it would be as well (depending on one's viewpoint) to start high or low since once can always move towards the other party. It is virtually impossible to move the other way. Whereas money was used as an illustration in the above example,*

other factors could be used – waiving of right to fourteen days' credit before payment of rent to gain a reduction, waiving of requirement to redecorate internally this year to gain acceptance of an increase and so on. In other areas we could use free stock, better delivery dates, extended credit, gifts, sale or return, and so on. The point about this tactic is to marshal all the 'benefits' in advance and then not to give any such CONCESSIONS away without gaining something in return.

Pre-emptive strike

Introduction

In some cases negotiators can be forgiven for wishing that they could conclude the encounter with one initial offer that is bound to gain agreement – literally a pre-emptive strike. In some instances, this tactic may be legitimate and successful. However, in others there are inherent dangers of antagonising the other side no matter how attractive an offer may seem to be – even to both parties.

Negotiation with representatives

In most employer–union negotiations, at least one side prefers the 'ritual dance' of original offer, rejection, consultation with members, alternative offer, etc. Even employers may be prepared to play along with this ritual since it does allow time for thought (and second thoughts) and possibly to introduce new topics for consideration – loss of payment for lateness, reduced breaks, stricter treatment of absenteeism, etc. Even if such items make no progress in year one they may be able to be re-introduced in year two or even to be introduced as a CONCESSION (ie. if we give you this, can you accept that?) during the encounter.

Irritation with the time that may be spent (or in some views 'wasted') on such negotiations may tempt management to try to make a pre-emptive offer – possibly one that they perceived to be slightly better than that which the employees' representatives thought they would achieve at the end of negotiations. The problem is this kind of approach can have a backlash.

Case study: What is the point of our efforts?

A factory manager was new and had been appointed as the previous year's wage negotiations were concluding. He felt that the several weeks of negotiations were very wasteful and decided that different tactics were required. Accordingly, when the time came he summoned the shop stewards and stated that he had no wish to waste several weeks' time on the ritual of offer, rejection and counter-offer. He stated that he was prepared to recommend an increase across the board of 6.5% which he felt was both the most the company could afford and also better than any offer that the representatives thought they would achieve. He put this offer to them and asked them to confirm it within three days.

He was somewhat nonplussed when they rejected the offer and his strategy collapsed into the normal negotiating procedure.

When, after three months, the talks were completed – with an award which was worth slightly less than the pre-emptive offer itself – he somewhat tetchily demanded of the shop steward 'Why on earth didn't you agree to my original offer?' He was told, 'Basically because if we had done so our members would have seen that there was no point to us being there – and indeed for them paying for us to be there. What would have been better would have been for you to have offered slightly less than your best offer, for us to have discussed it with our members and come back with a small increase (taking us to the figure which you originally offered) and you could then agree. You would have done your job and we would have been seen to have done ours.'

> **Key technique**
>
> The lesson to be drawn from this case study is that in negotiation not only should we ensure that we actively listen to the other side (i.e. listen to what they say, how they say it, note their body language, listen to what is not said, and so on) but also we should try to see things from their point of view. If we only ever see negotiation from our side then we run the risk – even with what seem to be attractive offers – of not gaining agreement simply because we have not appreciated what the other side requires from the encounter.

Provocation

Introduction

In the section headed AGGRAVATION we depicted an encounter with a cold caller who apparently felt he could obtain progress by losing his temper with his target. Other cold callers attempt to negotiate as if they were doing the target a favour, so much so that they can, by their own ineptitude, generate anger from the target. Provocation is hardly the best way of negotiating unless done deliberately to make the other side lose their TEMPER and to try to benefit from any lack of control in the ensuing heated encounter.

Case study: Poorly rated

'Please could I speak to the person who deals with your business rates.' (see key technique A)

'That's me.'

'We are a company of rates consultants with an excellent record in obtaining massive reductions and reassessments.' (See key technique B)

'Oh yes.'

'Our representative is in your area tomorrow and would like to make an appointment to see the person who deals with your rates.' (See key technique C)

'And what's the idea?'

'We will carry out a survey of the rates you are paying and show you how to save at least 10 per cent, but before doing so we do need an up front fee of £250 which will be more than covered by the savings we can show you.'

'I'm not interested in any service where I have to pay in advance' (See key technique D)

'We only insist on that because we have experienced problems with bad debts before and as a small organisation can be badly hit when people do not pay their bills.' (See key technique E)

The encounter on which this case study is based was recounted by Syd Rawcliffe in the ICSA journal 'Chartered Secretary' (then published under its former name of 'Administrator'). Having turned down the invitation his phone rang again later with the same opening spiel, and again, and again. In all he was contacted by the same woman ringing on behalf of the same organisation no less than five times in a single day. (See key techniques F, G and H)

Key techniques

A

The opening line indicates that it is a cold caller – they do not know who they wish to speak to and are fishing for a contact.

Solution
Find out who you wish to speak to. It is relatively easy to ring most organisations and say 'I have something to send to the person dealing with rates – but I want to address it to him or her personally – could you tell me their name and position?'. With this information the cold caller can at least make progress from the main switchboard to the office of the target. The other advantage, should the follow-up call actually get through to the target, is that the cold caller can say 'Good morning, Mr Jones, it's Peter Frost of Rate-U-Like here' creating at least some link between the parties. It may also create an impression that the caller may be someone the executive has met somewhere – they may even have asked them to call – so the stage is set.

Note: *If you want to be really devious you say 'I haven't got the name of the person dealing with your rates.'*
'It's Robinson.'
'Oh, I have their surname but not their first name.'

OR

'It's Anne.'
'Oh I know her first name – I wanted her surname.'

Both approaches indicate a previous contact so the cold call is not cold at all. One can come unstuck with names like Martin, Morris, Lewis, Lloyd etc. where the names can be either first or surnames!)

B

Anyone can claim this. In Syd's encounter, when he eventually saw the representative and asked for names of such referees, the information 'wasn't available'. This type of comment is patronising and insults the intelligence of the respondent - after all, if they are that good why do they need to cold call to gain business?

Solutions
(a) Obtain such recommendations - better still get a recommendation from a previously satisfied client addressed to the prospective client introducing the service. If the old client is known to the new client that link should at least ensure there is an opening gambit. In the absence of a link it might help if the recommendations were sent ahead.

(b) If recommendations are sent ahead they need to be personally addressed to the target. The follow-up (personally addressed) can then refer to the hard evidence already submitted. The ice has also been broken by the written contact which may also help the subsequent verbal discussion.

C

This shows an initial lack of concentration whilst the second part of the sentence may be seen as the lie it probably is. The respondent has already stated that he deals with the rates so implying that there is a lack of knowledge of this point indicates poor administration and efficiency that is hardly a good indication of the service that may be expected should the organisation be retained to carry out the work.

Of course, implied within the comment is the criticism that whoever is doing the job now is not doing it economically. It may be true but the point needs tactful handling as part of the negotiations – more tact than is likely from this caller.

Added to which the suggestion that someone will be 'in your area' is so corny as to be deserving of being ignored as an almost certain lie by most respondents – once more the respondent is entitled to feel he is being patronised.

Solutions
(a) When the respondent stated that she dealt with the rates, the immediate follow-up question should have been 'Could I possibly have your name?' which should then have been written by the caller in large letters on the pad next to the telephone number being called.

Her name should have been used during the conversation to try and build a rapport.

(b) It might be more advisable to suggest that the caller attempts to make an appointment 'at a convenient time' rather than attempting to con the respondent who, if she has been in business any length of time, will have heard such a spiel many times before.

(c) Avoid treating respondents as if they have no intelligence. Such is the growth in the reliance on cold calling in this way that most businesses receive such calls weekly. The common hidden message that 'we can run your business more cost-effectively than you' is a hook that may be correct but needs to be tempered with tact.

D and E

Virtually every business has had this problem some time in their existence. The fact that the caller has had problems with bad debts is his problem and nothing to do with a prospective client.

Solutions

(a) Such a service if it has faith in its ability should really be prepared to deal on the basis of a split of the savings – in other words 'putting its money where its mouth is'.

(b) In addition, in stating the problem at this early stage in the encounter the organisation is providing all the wrong signals. Few if any businessmen or women with any experience will view this as anything other than pretty sharp practice.

F and G

This is a hardly a good advert for the efficiency of the organisation. Pretty obviously the caller is someone who, given inadequate briefing regarding making such a call and inadequate training in handling people, has been handed some numbers and told to 'try to get me an interview with someone on this list'. Ensuring that those already called are crossed off the list or, only if successful, are passed to the next stage would help both sides immeasurably – it should also ensure that provocation does not destroy a previous successful call.

Solutions

(a) Proper product and service training so that the caller knows what is on offer

(b) Adequate training in how to make and progress the call with due regard for the susceptibilities of the respondent (who if they were not annoyed by the first or second calls will be getting pretty annoyed by the fifth interruption.

(c) A proper system for making such calls so that each has a slip with the target's name plus as much information about their organisation as possible so that the caller can speak from some experience of their set-up. Where a call is successful, the slip should be moved to a 'follow-up' file with any additional information added to it. Where the call is unsuccessful, it should be moved to a 'failed' file but before doing so the number should be deleted from all lists so that there is no further wasted call(s). (Of course it may be required to move it to a 'try again in six months' file rather than writing off as a complete loss.)

H

The caller would not be human if, being paid on the basis of a commission on successful calls, as most people making these calls are, his disappointment at receiving another 'no sale' message did not colour the way in which he deals with the calls. Each call tends to become a repetitive spiel with less and less commitment and enthusiasm.

Solutions

(a) Encourage callers to write their own script and determine their own way of doing things subject to proper (and not exaggerated) claims regarding the product/service.

(b) Monitor how each call is handled and suggest ways of improving the patter. This is particularly important with those new to the job whose enthusiasm and lack of awareness of the reaction of the call's recipient may impair their efforts.

Note: *In some parts of the European Union such cold calling is already banned and there are currently plans to extend such a prohibition. Reputable organisations in the UK already abide by codes of conduct for cold calling, whilst charities are governed by legislation on the subject.*

Quid pro quo

Introduction

The old Latin phrase 'quid pro quo' (literally 'something for something') can be translated as 'this for that' or, more colloquially, 'You scratch my back and I'll scratch yours'. Experienced negotiators advise that one should try never to give away any advantage without getting something in return. This tactic could also be entitled 'If I...' that is 'If I agree to reduce the price increase from £2.60 to £2.50 I want you to agree to pay within seven days, rather than fourteen days, of invoice', the inference being that 'if not then I can't see a way of giving you the advantageous price'.

Valuing concessions

The rule above can perhaps be refined to suggest that anything you concede should be of less value than what you gain in return – in other words that you should concede what has little value to you to gain something that has greater value. The difficulty (which can also be a potential advantage) is that items may have different values to the two parties in a negotiation. If the concession has little value to the person conceding and greater value to the other side this is extremely valuable to the person conceding; conversely, if a required concession has greater value to the person asked to concede than to the person making the request this may pose difficulties. It is perhaps stating the obvious to say that one should try to discover the value of the item requested.

This question of attempting to determine the value of various aspects contained within a negotiation encounter is all-important. Items that we value lowly may have an enhanced value to the other side. If we are prepared to give way on the item we need to have in our mind the perceived value placed upon it by the other side. Trying to ascertain this can be difficult but is vital. Conversely something that we value highly (e.g. being paid on time) may actually be of relatively low value to the other side.

Case study : Rate for the job

An author had been approached to act as a consultant editor for a new loose-leaf publication. He had not performed such a task before and, although he could estimate the time involved, he had no idea of the fee that he should ask.

'What would you charge us for this service?' asked the publisher's representative.

'That's very difficult as I can't work out how much time this would involve. I meant to ask (name of author doing similar work on another title) how much she charged but I couldn't contact her before this meeting. How much do you normally pay such editors? Is it a flat fee or royalty or a bit of both?'

The representative hesitated but then stated a figure used on a similar publication. The fact that the author had inferred that he knew a mutual contact, placed some pressure on the publisher's representative to quote a reasonably accurate figure. Left to himself, the author would have quoted an altogether lower figure.

> **Key technique**
>
> 1. If in doubt let the other side make the running. It is often said that many people tend to undervalue themselves and further that more organisations go out of business because they charge too little rather than charge too much. The perception of value of the other side is all-important and we need to be able to gain at least some indication of that value. Almost certainly their figure will be pitched 'low' but at least this should mean we know where to aim our counter-offer.
>
> 2. The other problem with this kind of negotiation is that whilst a one-off fixed fee may look attractive now, a royalty agreement might be better in the long run if the manual is a best-seller.

Continuing concessions

Another problem that arises with concessions concerns the time-span of operation. If both concessions are ongoing there may be little of concern, but if the continuation of one concession depends on the status quo being maintained there can be a danger that it could be lost due to some change.

Case study: No insurance guarantee

A manager was concerned that due to fluctuations in the insurance market, the premiums being requested by the insurers tended to vary widely regardless of the claims incidence of his vehicle fleet. One year when a good record coincided with a good market there was no pressure for any increased premium. Rather than pressing for a reduction he suggested that the premium be increased by 10 per cent but that this should be taken into account in the future when the claims incidence and/or market force might move against the company. This was agreed and worked well for three years until the director of the insurer changed and his successor was unwilling to continue this innovative approach.

> **Key technique**
>
> Being innovative in negotiating can be valuable. In addition to posing unusual solutions to situations, the 'oddball' suggestion may so confuse the other side that they agree virtually without thought.

Examples of 'quids' for 'quos'

(a) 'Yes, we will pay overtime at double rate but only for the second and third hours worked each day and providing the employee has completed a full day's work already.'

(b) 'Yes, we will shave a penny a widget off the price but only in exchange for a firm order for 10,000 units signed today, payment to be within fourteen days of invoice.'

(c) 'Yes, you can have a credit note for £100 plus VAT against our invoice dated XXX but only on condition that we have a cheque for the net amount immediately.'

(d) 'Yes we will stop noisy building works between the hours of ten and twelve and two and four as long as you agree that we can get on with our work, some of which may be noisy, at all other times.'

(e) 'Yes, we will return to work as long as you agree to review our requirements within seven days.'

and so on.

Quite deliberately each of the above examples begins with the word 'Yes'. Yes is a positive sign, a sign that the parties are in agreement. Even though in each case there are strings attached to the agreement, the immediate signal by using the word 'Yes' is that 'We are in agreement; there's only a few bits of nitty gritty to sort out now'.

SARAH

Introduction

SARAH is a friendly and helpful import from the USA and although she was originated for use in selling, her principles apply equally to all one-to-one relationships including negotiations. Adopting her five-stage recommendations should enable us to achieve better understanding and rapport with those with whom we have to interface. SARAH stands for Smile, Active listening, Repeat comments, Act with empathy and Handle with care respectively.

The SARAH checklist

Smile

Whilst it is true that a smile can be insincere and merely used for effect, the initial reaction to a smiling person is to smile in return – thus generating at least a basic rapport. A smile can put the other party at their ease and indicates an informal approach, which tends to relax most people and can have unexpected results. Whilst not suggesting we should trivialise matters or always smile when it would be inappropriate, smiling also relaxes your vocal chords. Because your vocal chords are relaxed your tone will be relaxed; because you are relaxed the other party is more likely to become relaxed and a rapport is more likely to be created.

Smiling may also indicate sincerity although obviously this too may be false and is reminiscent of the advice to the would-be sales representative; 'If you can fake sincerity you have it made'.

Active listening

The corollary to ceasing to hammer home one's point of view to the exclusion of that of the listener is to listen more. Hearing is purely a mechanical act, whereas listening entails active consideration of what is both said and left unsaid. Only if we listen to both what is and is not said will we gain the real views of the other party. The longer people talk the more they reveal of their true feelings. This may mean that negotiations last longer – but the pay off may be more WIN:WIN situations. In Active listening perhaps we should also include the need to listen to or watch body language since the way a person's body is held or moves can provide clues to the way they are really thinking – a guide which may be entirely different from the words being uttered. Body language (voice tone, type of language, expression, the way the body is held and so on) can contribute as much as 90% of the message being conveyed.

Repeat comments

This is a device designed to show that the caller (or respondent) has understood exactly what the respondent (or caller) has said and is essential to ensure both parties understand the other precisely. Repeating key sentences or comments in their own words

(a) helps fix the details of the matter in the mind

(b) helps check that what has been received was what was meant

(c) engenders a rapport and understanding between the two parties

(d) leads to really accurate communication (that is, the accurate comprehension of the points by both parties).

This should remove all possibility of misunderstandings during negotiations. It should not be overlooked that repeating key sentences or agreements – and making notes of them – can help avoid the possibility of one party exploiting the MEMORY FAILURE tactic, – that is, deliberately mis-remembering what was previously agreed.

Act with empathy

This entails showing the other party that you understand and appreciate their feelings and motivation. This does not mean you necessarily agree with them but does indicate that you recognise – even respect – their point of view. Even though there may be no meeting of minds on points of dispute, at least the relationship is there – demonstrating that one understands the viewpoint of the other.

Handle the subject matter with appreciation of the feelings of the other party

More specifically, we should handle the subject matter with an appreciation of the feelings of the other party. We can, of course, only do this if we try to place ourselves in their position. If we do then we may be able to understand their viewpoint – even though we may not be able to agree with it. Understanding it may enable us to make a suggestion whereby they are able to see a way of agreeing to what we want.

Case study: Takeover

A predator wished to take control of an unquoted target company. It knew the price it wanted to pay and believed that such a price would easily secure acceptance by the target company's shareholders. It also knew that the directors of the target wished to remain independent and would firmly resist the merger or takeover if they could. The predator was convinced, however, that, despite the attitude of the directors, the right price would win the day, that even if the target's directors fought they would lose. Nonetheless acceptance by the target (thus making it an agreed bid) would be preferable to a battle, so the chairman of the predator company approached the chairman of the target.

'I wanted to have a word with you in confidence.'

'Oh yes.'

'As you know, we acquired the shares formerly held by [name] recently and we feel we would like to make a full bid.'

'I see.'

'I don't suppose it comes as too great a surprise. The point is that we can offer either a good price or a very good price for the company.'

'How come?'

'We don't believe a hostile bid is in anyone's interests and it will be very expensive. We are certain we would win but both companies would have to pay some very large bills from two sets of professional advisers – and a disputed bid will be very time consuming during which time little may be done to drive either company forward. It seems to me that it would be far better for us to bid at the level you would feel happy to recommend to your shareholders.'

'There's a great deal of sense in that. What figure did you have in mind?'

'£4 per share.'

'I see,' replied the target chairman, thinking to himself that at that price it was almost a PRE-EMPTIVE STRIKE – the most recent estimate of the value of each share being only £2.20.

'I think you have to agree that it's a generous figure but what I'd like to suggest is that we bid £3.80.'

'What happened to the other 20p?'

'That's where you and your board come in. I am sure you would like to be seen to be serving your shareholders well. If we bid £3.80 and then we both say we're having talks, after a few days we can put out a joint statement saying that you will recommend the bid to your shareholders provided it is at £4 per share which we are prepared to pay – then everyone will be happy.'

> *Note:* *This assumes both companies are unquoted. Quoted companies are governed by the City Code rules which could exclude such an arrangement even though it could be argued that it is in the interests of both sets of shareholders.*

Key technique

No-one likes to lose so if we can offer those who will really be the losers a way of salving their pride or proving their worth we may be able to appear to grant a WIN:WIN situation in what is in reality a LOSE:WIN encounter.

Settling old scores

Introduction

A high proportion of individual negotiation encounters are actually part of a chain of related encounters such as a buyer and her regular supplier (and vice versa), an employee (or representative) and his employer, a tenant and its landlord and so on. In such circumstances there are two ways of regarding the encounter:

(a) as part of a continuum, one step along a long path

(b) as a one-off.

Continuum

In the case of the continuum, it is recognised that there is a long-term relationship and the best way of both getting what they want from the relationship is for each negotiation to be settled so that both parties achieve something and the relationship itself is left reasonably intact for future encounters and negotiations. This may be particularly true of a personal relationship such as that of employer:employee. If it is true that the purpose of management is to encourage people to succeed then negotiations regarding pay and training, etc., should support endeavours and concentrate on successes (by demonstrating belief and confidence in the employee in financial terms as well as words) rather than using failures to militate against a pay increase. Achieving a low level of pay increases may appear economically sound but this is hardly true if the 'best' employees then leave or work less effectively because they feel 'cheated' as a result of the negotiations.

One-off

Regarding each encounter as a one-off means no recognition is granted to the fact that taking advantage of favourable terms this time around may be counter-productive in the future. Those who feel angry about a negotiation where they were 'bested' may have long memories. Next time around they may have an opportunity to settle an old score.

Case study: He who laughs last, laugh lasts

A rent review was due. Before the tenant had conducted any negotiations, the landlord applied to have the matter settled by a third party, ignoring the fact that the lease terms stipulated a process that had not taken place. Despite remonstrations by the tenant, and attempts to negotiate, the third party determined the rent. The tenant felt very angry about the whole way the review had been conducted.

Some time later the landlord wished to restructure the lease so that it would be more valuable as he wished to sell his interest. He approached the tenant who refused initial offers and pushed the price very high. On every occasion when the negotiations were taking place the tenant reminded the other side of the harsh way that they had been treated during the review. This 'sore point' routine eventually led to the landlord paying far more to obtain the restructure than he had anticipated.

History remembered

Sometimes settling old scores can take a considerable time – but those who have been (as they see it) unfairly treated often have very long memories. Being treated badly tends to stick in many people's memories for far longer than memories of when they have been treated well. The inability to square matters can act as a spur to action when the opportunity arises even if this may result in action which is not entirely in one's own interests.

Case study: The elephant dictum

When young and inexperienced a manager had been subjected to 'sharp' practice by a representative of a photocopier company. He discovered on later investigation that he had been lied to and generally conned into signing an order for an additional machine that was not really necessary.

In later life he was often in the position of advising people about buying or leasing succeeding generations of copiers and, never forgetting his bad experience, never once did he recommend that company's machines – always pointing out that their terms needed to be investigated thoroughly as did the statements made by their representatives.

Shock tactics

Introduction

We tend to negotiate many times a day in our personal lives. Most of these encounters are informal and indeed we may not even think of them as negotiation – simply logical extensions of conversations. Even in business life we may negotiate without thinking:

A: 'I simply haven't got time to finish all your letters this afternoon; I must leave on time.'

B: 'Well, do the first seven today and leave the others till tomorrow but could you stay late tomorrow night as we need to get that report out.'

A: 'Sure, I can stay as late as you want provided I can have a couple of hours off at midday to get my shopping.'

B: 'Fine, let's work to that arrangement.'

A and B have gone through a process of negotiation which one could almost call 'You scratch my back and I'll scratch yours' and this catchphrase probably describes the majority of encounters where negotiations take place in such an informal setting (see QUID PRO QUO).

However, in certain circumstances such niceties of 'I win a point, you win a point' may be laid aside and it may be deemed necessary to use tactics that depend for their success on the shock that they give to their target.

Case study: Changing the format

In the 1980s when the print unions were strong a publisher had been forced to concede annual wage increases that exceeded the increase in profitability of the company. When the first signs of recession started it was obvious that this arrangement could not continue. The managing director decided different tactics to the usual whittling down of high demands to barely affordable levels would have to be employed. When the mother and father of chapel (shops stewards in that industry) attended a meeting to commence the normal round of discussions, he swiftly came to the point.

'What increase are you asking for this year?'

'9% on basic pay rates plus a reduction from 40 to 39 hours.'

'I see. So that is basically an 11.5% increase since presumably you want the same pay for 39 hours as you would get for 40.'

'Yes.'

'Fine. In that case we will agree to the new base rate and the reduction in hours. However the effect of that is that we need to shrink the workforce by 10% so if you want those new rates of pay and hours we need to identify 35 people to be made redundant. The normal agreed arrangements are last in first out and we have compiled this list of 35 names. You will note that as two of you are relatively recent joiners your names are included on the list. Obviously, I would like to keep this matter confidential and would ask you to think about it and return tomorrow with your views.'

The following day the representatives returned with an alternative suggestion that wage rates be increased by 5% and the hours be left unchanged. The MD's reaction was equally firm.

'In that case, we will still need to lose ten people to pay for the additional wage costs.'

> Note: This occurred in the early 1980s. Current legislation would outlaw the concept of producing a list of names without there having been negotiation regarding the possibility of redundancy.

Risk

The tactics used in the above case study carry a high risk. It could backfire and with a militant union lead to industrial action, although this is less likely now than it was then. However, ensuring that the representatives within an industry where technological change was forcing major changes in working practices, recognised the economic facts of life, particularly when two of those negotiating were personally involved, was deemed worth the risk. Of course the tactics could only be used in their most 'shocking' form once. The following year, the negotiations were conducted along the same 'If you want x% we must lose Y people' basis and this then became the norm.

'High risk' can be said to lead to 'high gain' and 'low risk' to 'low gain'. In situations like the above what needs to be recognised is the continuing relationship – the need to negotiate repeatedly – ie. we need to consider the reaction of those who we 'best' when the terms are in our favour, when the terms move in their favour. Alternatively, we can take the attitude that we will make what we can whilst we can and suffer the consequences when the terms move against us. (See SETTLING OLD SCORES.)

Dissent

Silence can be an effective tactic. Whilst it is often said that 'silence signifies assent', very often in a negotiation encounter silence is taken to indicate dissent. The person who can keep silent places pressure on the other party to fill the void by speaking. The classic scenario is the television interview where the subject is being grilled. If instead of arguing and even, as in some celebrated instances, trying to walk out on the interview (albeit a tactic rendered impossible in at least one encounter because of a voice mike connected to their clothing), the interviewee had simply said 'No comment' or 'I have no wish to comment on that', the interview would need to be brought to an end as a silent 'talking head' makes even less effective television than does a talking 'talking head'. Whilst informed comment may be valuable, it is confrontation that leads to peak viewing figures.

Case study: Costly silence

An agent had been instructed to get as much for the letting as possible and had one potential tenant who was very interested in the property and had put in an offer. The landlord had told the agent that he would accept the figure put forward by the tenant. The agent rang the tenant and said that he had been chatting about the offer to the landlord and felt they should 'touch base' with the tenant again to check developments. He then paused.

After a few seconds the tenant was tempted by the silence and said that he had also been thinking things over and would be prepared to increase his offer slightly. The agent simply said 'Mmmm' and kept quiet. The tenant then increased his offer to above the figure that had been stated to be acceptable by the landlord.

Had the tenant remained silent – or even simply replied to the phone call with 'What had you in mind?' – he could have saved himself £200 (or in reality, since it was a review covering the following five years, £1000 over the period). In addition, his too-swift agreement meant that at the next review the starting point for those negotiations would be £200 higher than would otherwise have been the case.

Pressure

When used to conversations akin to a tennis match – one person 'serving' a sentence to be matched by another 'returning' their view – sometimes simply waiting for a comment can put considerable pressure on the other side (which is particularly true of telephone conversations). This is not meant to suggest that we should respond to every negotiating comment with a silence that may be taken as insulting, but that if the other party is at all rude, aggressive or abusive (or indeed all three) then it may be better to keep quiet and let them run themselves out of steam.

Case study: And?

A famous actress was confronted in her dressing room by a fan irate at some action that she had taken. For a full three minutes he ranted at her, remonstrating at her action, criticising her and inferring that she had taken leave of her senses. At a suitable pause in the diatribe she commented 'And?'

He started again, repeating much of what he had already said, but more swiftly ran out of comments, at which point she said 'And?'

But he had had enough and rushed from her dressing room. Effectively she had won the encounter with two words and two long silences. In heated situations allowing the other party to unload their whole comments without comment of one's own is equivalent to the army firing off the whole of its ammunition in an initial barrage and then having nothing in reserve. An initial barrage of half the length followed by silence poses the enemy with a dilemma – have they run out or is it a ploy?

Using the silent approach is akin to leaving the other side to 'punch cotton wool', which can be very frustrating for the irate party.

Splitting the difference

Introduction

Where two sides have a common interest, the only problem they may have to determine is where to draw the line of agreement between their respective 'best' positions ie. the compromise with which they can both live. However in some cases negotiation may be more concerned with minimising the loss to each side. In such a situation the best approach may be to pause and consider exactly what we have got and what we want.

The judgment of Solomon

In the ancient world, when faced with two women both claiming to be the mother of a child, Solomon proposed cutting the child in half and giving half to each claimant.

In negotiation where half a loaf may be better than no loaf but is nowhere near as appealing as a whole loaf, the problem comes not so much with agreeing to the solution as in positioning where the split should fall. In terms of a negotiation encounter the position of the cut can make all the difference between an acceptable fall-back position and an unacceptable deal.

The problem with splitting the difference is that often, by the time the suggestion is made, the parties may have moved from their original positions anyway. In such a circumstance, if one feels that splitting (literally agreeing a figure halfway between the two points) gives away too much, reverting to the previous position and splitting the difference from those points may be more sensible (although providing no guarantee of agreement of course).

Case study: The moving cut

A landlord had asked for a new rent of £26,000 – an increase of £11,000 on the previous rent. The tenant had resisted and argued and eventually been forced to move her offer to £20,000 whilst the landlord had come down to £22,500. The landlord then suggested that they split the difference at £21,250, but the tenant pointed out that she had already moved £5,000 whilst the landlord had moved only £3,500.

Whilst she was not averse to gaining agreement without involving third parties by splitting the difference, she felt it should be on the basis of the original positions of the two parties, ie. at a figure of £20,500. This would mean only a movement of £750 from the figure the landlord seemed prepared to accept.

Key technique

Another point covered by this case study is the pressure to accept the marginal movement. 'There's only £750 between us – can't you agree that?' is the tenant's line, ignoring the fact that originally there was £11,000 between them and £3,500 has already been conceded. In some instances, faced with such circumstances the parties actually finish up splitting the difference OF the difference – in the above example agreeing to split the £750 and making the agreed rent £20,875!

Arithmetic

The concept of the difference split is mathematically logical but there its logic ceases. All sorts of other factors are inherent in negotiations. Nevertheless, 'splitting the difference' to gain an agreed solution is very widespread, not least since it enables the parties to cease their discussions and move on with neither actually 'losing' and both gaining something from the encounter – the classic WIN:WIN situation.

Take it or leave it (or 'Hobson's choice')

Introduction

The Hobson in this instance is the person who offered only two options – 'Take it or leave it – that's all there is'. Of course, this may not be very satisfying to us as a buyer as generally most people like to feel that they have got a good deal. Perhaps one of the salutary lessons for negotiators to learn may be how to make it appear to the other party that they have got a good deal! Usually our estimation of a good deal is that we got a good price, but price is not the only criteria by which we judge whether a deal is good or not.

No negotiation

It is perhaps inappropriate to include a tactic of non-negotiation in a book on negotiation but there are ways in which the tactic can be used positively. In essence, the theory echoes Henry Ford's answer to those who wanted coloured cars: 'They can have any colour they like as long as it's black'. If you as a customer walk into a shop looking for a product and the assistant, having checked the stockroom, tells you 'We've only got one in stock', it is unlikely that any negotiating will help you move the price your way. Indeed, in many instances (not so much in a shop), the vendor might be able to move the price, or some other element, for example, delivery cost or time, against you, simply because the item – if there really is only one – has a rarity value.

The fact that you were unable to move the price your way will not necessarily stop you boasting of your purchase 'I got the last one' as though this was something other than luck that you walked in and asked for an item just after they sold the penultimate one and just before the first unsuccessful enquirer!

Using the device

Of course, the shop assistant knows the true position regarding the stock which the customer does not. Replying 'Yes but we've only got one' (even if there are many) places an onus on the customer to snap it up before the sole remaining item is bought by someone else. This is akin to the device of placing a number of products in a dump bin in a shop with a sign 'Last few – only £X'. Since most people cannot resist a bargain (or what they perceive as a bargain) such 'last few' products often disappear very quickly (only to be replaced by the retailer once the coast is clear). This is the classic 'WIN-WIN' of negotiation. Both sides are happy – the customer thinks he has a bargain (even if he does not) and the retailer clears the stock.

Case study: Pile it high – and sell it expensive

In one of London's street markets there was a sweet shop and outside a stall operated by the owner of the shop. The shop was nearly always fairly empty whereas the stall was always crowded with onlookers and buyers. The shop owner was a gifted salesman whose patter was well worth listening to for entertainment value alone. He would pick up products from the piles in front of him with two careful fingers (thus inferring that the product was very valuable, fragile, high quality etc.) and pile box after box up his arm. He would then add up the prices and start slashing the total for the whole selection. Inevitably once his spiel slowed there would be customers.

I was always fascinated by the spiel and the quick-talking salesman – even more so since in looking round the shop I had worked out that buying the same selection in the shop as he had running up his arm, could actually cost you less than buying from the stall. But then you didn't have the entertainment of his spiel and the often hilarious customer/salesman interface!

Latent negotiation

Similar logic to that behind the 'dump bin' and the confectionery salesman's arm of products exists in the concept of limiting sales to customers or callers. Indeed the stallholder would often say as part of his spiel 'This is such a good offer I can only let you have one per person.' In addition, mail order adverts in the national press often stipulate 'only one per household'. Since generally we understand that to be successful most businesses need to sell as many products as possible, indicating that the business is prepared to trade with us on such a limited basis raises in the mind of the customer a perception of quality or rarity (or both) that places pressure on them to conclude the deal at the price stated. We can call this latent negotiation since one party is being negotiated with by the other, but instead of the normal verbal argument and discussion, the negotiations are being carried out via written messages and perceptions.

Postscript: If times were a bit slow for the confectionery salesman a regular customer in the crowd would sometimes be the first to buy. I thought he ate a great deal of confectionery until I bumped into him in the shop unloading the bags he had just 'bought'. Things are not always what they seem.

Temper – false

Introduction

In TEMPER – REAL we deal with the situation where it is necessary to allow time for a real loss of temper to cool simply since until it does it is unlikely that either negotiation will make any progress. There are situations however where it may be useful to 'lose' one's temper deliberately.

The effect

Losing one's temper for effect is a dangerous ploy – and it may be impossible to reuse it with the same opponent. However, one instance of 'loss of temper' may create an impression that here is a 'difficult negotiator', which may be of benefit in repeated negotiations. As well as such a long-term signal, the temper loss sends signals to the other side which can include:

(a) I feel so very strongly about this that you had better back off and think again about your strategy.

(b) I require to be treated with respect and regard which has not been present so far.

(c) You have not fully appreciated the effect of what you are asking.

(d) You are assuming I am a fool.

These messages are all negative and could have the effect of stalling the negotiation, although of course this may be what the user of the device wants – possibly to play for time, to put pressure on the other side, or simply to demonstrate that they too are tough negotiators.

Side effects

The problems associated with losing one's temper, even deliberately, are that:

(a) unless controlled, it can indicate that the 'loser' is not actually in control of him or herself. The voice tends to move up in pitch and become shrill, etc.

(b) it can silence the onlookers who do not really know how to react (again this can be intended by the 'loser' who may be able to gain agreement to his desired result by placing his opponents under the duress generated by his outburst)

(c) it may be difficult to regain one's poise without it being obvious that the whole matter had been staged for a purpose.

Case study: Pressure

A customer had experienced considerable but intermittent trouble with an electrical product bought from a store and rang the store to enquire what to do about it. 'Bring it in and we will replace it' was the advice given over the phone.

However, on visiting the store, the reaction from the assistant was somewhat different. The customer explained the fault and that it was intermittent and the product was currently faulty. The assistant gave the product several slaps with his hand and it began to work perfectly.

'There, it's working.'

'But the problem is intermittent. It will work for a while and then stop. That's the whole point, as I explained on the phone yesterday.'

'We'll have to send it for repair.'

'I don't want it repaired. I want it replaced as your telephonist promised when I rang yesterday.'

'No, replacement isn't on. We'll repair it.'

At this point the customer standing in the middle of a crowded nationally known chain store deliberately raised his voice so that the attention of the surrounding customers was drawn to the dispute. In a loud voice he demanded to know: 'Are you telling me that having telephoned your store to tell them of this problem and being told that you would exchange a faulty product, and having made a special trip to return this item, you will now not honour that promise?'

'Well, I…'

'I have shown you that the item is faulty and your reaction was to give a delicate electrical item two or three hefty knocks and say you've cured it.'

'That's all…'

'Fetch the manager here – I want this sorted out NOW. If what you say is really how you wish to treat your customers, I find such an attitude is entirely unsatisfactory.'

Key technique

Since the customer was quite deliberately calling the attention of the onlookers to the situation by virtually shouting his comments, the store staff had a real problem – not just of dealing with him, but of trying to avoid the 'knock on' effect that his comments could have on other potential customers.

Solutions

(a) Avoid the action that led to such a situation (i.e. proper training in customer complaint conversion for the assistant).

(b) Clearly defined procedures for dealing with such problems.

(c) Moving the complaining customer off the sales floor to a confidential office so that the pressure of the onlookers is removed. Here the customer was able to use those watching as additional negotiators on his side. Indeed, one even came up to him during the encounter to encourage him to stick out for his rights.

Temper – real

Introduction

Most negotiations are conducted in an atmosphere of calm and reason even though both parties may be striving to obtain the best they can from the encounter. In some circumstances, however such rational discussion can degenerate into a heated row where one or both parties lose their temper. The most important point to remember about temper is that 'He who loses his temper loses the point'.

Moving forward

In some instances (such as employer – employee relationships) where the negotiations are just one incident within a lasting relationship, the fact that temper has been lost simply means that the negotiations cannot continue. Since that is the aim we need to have a policy for handling temper.

Strategy for dealing with temper loss

1. Remain calm at all times. Once two tempers clash then it is unlikely that any consensus will emerge, and the situation will almost certainly degenerate. (It should be noted that in some instances if one party remains calm this can actually be even more aggravating to the other. Failure to generate a heated response is akin to punching cotton wool and can have the effect of generating even more heat.)

2. Note facts or opposing views without immediately commenting. Commenting hastily may merely inflame the situation, whilst the longer the person can talk without being challenged, the more they may be able to reduce the pressure they feel. (Indeed, in negotiations, keeping the other talking is valuable as more and more of their case will be revealed. As Churchill said 'Jaw jaw is better than war war.')

3. Keep the person talking and explaining the cause of the temper loss, whilst asking neutral questions to try and uncover as much of the case, or cause of concern, as possible.

4. Attempt to relax the person by means of refreshment, smoking, etc. Although there may be a temptation to force a conclusion to the negotiation whilst the other party may be thinking less than clearly this may be counter-productive in the long run.

5. Declare a recess or adjournment of the negotiations. This should allow time for reconsideration as well as for the temper to cool.

6. Provide refreshments, thereby diverting attention to a neutral act. This may provide valuable calming time.

7. After the initial flow of words generated by the loss of temper has ceased, re-check and correct the facts as already discovered and noted. The purpose is to prepare an accurate résumé of the state of the negotiations when the temper was lost. If the party disagrees with the notes, alter them without comment until an agreed version is available.

8. Leave as much time as possible for the calming process. The longer the time taken the better as the more likely it is that the temper may subside.

Failure to achieve comprehension

It should not be overlooked that some people find considerable difficulty in expressing themselves clearly. This can mean that the other party then has a failure to understand them or the points they are making. In turn this is frustrating for the original person whose irritation can swiftly turn to anger directed at the other party although self-generated. In such circumstances the onus is very much on the other party to try to put their opponent's case for them. Unless they do, no progress can be made so this is in their interests. One way of doing this is by using the five-pronged approach set out in SARAH.

Backlash

Negotiation is likely to be most successful when both parties recognise the rights of and respect the other. If such rights are infringed then it may be hardly surprising if temper results. In such circumstances it is unlikely – even if time is left for the temper to cool – that one's aims are to be achieved.

Case study: Manners maketh the deal

A team of union representatives knew that negotiations were always conducted in the board room. On one occasion, having arrived early at the company's premises, the full-time officials did not bother to stop at reception but marched straight into the board room and sat down – one of them in the chair usually occupied by the managing director who chaired the meetings and negotiations.

So angry was the MD when he entered the room to discover the situation that progress on the negotiations was completely halted.

Key technique

The action of the MD in the above case study may be regarded by some as childish. Whether or not that is the case, he felt very strongly that the union representatives had behaved with a total lack of manners and politeness and the result was that no progress was made. This hiatus was not in the interests of either side but since the union were trying to obtain benefit concessions as well as a wage increase, the loss of progress was of greater value and concern to them than it was to the MD who held the power to grant the concessions. Politeness and a recognition of the susceptibilities of the other side cost nothing, and unless the purpose is deliberate aggravation may be pointless.

Terms

Introduction

Very often business negotiations fail for the simplest of reasons – either that one party did not understand the terms of the other party or that there were no terms to act as guidance in the event of dispute. Both discrepancies need to be addressed. It seems odd to think that some organisations having gone to considerable efforts to make good quality products or provide services, then fail to ensure that their business is protected by terms which will enable them to be paid the correct amount at the correct time.

In feint

Many organisations prefer to print their terms feint and in very small type on the reverse of an order, or acknowledgement of order form or similar. Whilst this is understandable it has several shortcomings

(a) Because the type used is so small it is very difficult to read – a problem made far more difficult by being printed in feint.

(b) Being in small type many people believe that the supplier may have something to hide.

(c) The language used is often legalistic and jargon-ridden.

(d) The presentation militates against a customer ever reading the terms and thus if there is a query it may tend to occur after the event leading to a dispute rather than negotiation.

Legislation

This is an acute problem for the supplier dealing with members of the public – where the contention set out in (b) above is very widespread. Such suppliers need to be aware of the Unfair Contract Terms legislation details of which are set out in the following checklist.

Unfair Contract Terms

As a result of a European Union directive the UK introduced new legislation aimed at protecting individual consumers from terms applied by suppliers to business. The Unfair Terms in Consumer Contracts Regulations 1994 came into effect on 1 July 1995 and applies only to contracts between a supplier and an individual(s) NOT to contracts between suppliers or organisations.

All terms not individually negotiated between supplier and consumer are subject to the legislation.

Classifications

There are two levels of classifications of terms:

(a) core terms (which relate to the main subject matter of the contract)
(b) other administrative terms.

Core terms must be subjected to a plain English test. That is they must be expressed in plain English and if not they will not be binding.

Administrative terms must be subjected BOTH to the plain English test and to an 'unfairness' test.

Good faith

In addition, terms must be presented in a format which shows good faith by the supplier. This will include:

(a) the bargaining strength of the parties (that is, does the consumer have the ability to change the terms or is he presented with them as a fait accompli)

   Note: Using a phrase such as 'fait accompli' would presumably breach the plain English test under this legislation!

(b) whether any inducement was offered to gain agreement to the term
(c) whether the customer's order was in any way special or a one-off
(d) the way in which the consumer has been dealt with by the supplier.

In addition, all the other contract terms will be considered in relation to this 'good faith' test.

If there are unfair terms?

Then the term will not be binding on the consumer. However in order to obtain such a relaxation, the consumer will need to obtain a court order.

An appeal can be made to the Director General of Fair Trading to declare a term unfair and request that it be suppressed.

Only if the rest of the contract can exist without the unfair term(s) can it remain in being.

Avoiding dispute negotiation

Although, in the event of dispute, the supplier may be able to refer to the terms, if they are in small virtually unreadable type this may not avoid argument. It may be preferable therefore to stress the salient features of the terms from the outset. Then, although it will not necessarily avoid dispute and consequent negotiation, at least an instant answer can be 'You will recall we brought this matter to your attention when we took your order'.

The important feature in drafting terms is to ensure that they are fair (a legal requirement as far as terms related to members of the public in any case, as set out above).

Case study: Missing terms lose negotiations

This was the second order placed by the customer. The first had been a somewhat rushed order for Christmas gifts and the second was in response to a discount flier the company had produced to try to generate trade in the low demand part of their year. Following its standard practice, the company had produced and invoiced 10% over the number of items ordered. The customer telephoned to query this.

'I am very surprised to see that the order that I requested for delivery by 1 April was delivered late without any apology and in addition you have charged me for overs.'

'That is in accordance with our standard conditions of trade shown on our catalogue. I'll send you a copy.' (See key technique 1.)

After receiving the catalogue, the customer telephoned again.

'I queried your charging for the overs on my second order, and the late delivery, and you have sent me your catalogue. However, I would point out that your discount flier makes no reference to any such conditions. In addition, you have ignored the fact that the order was late delivered, whilst, in reading through the catalogue, I have realised that you overcharged my first order last Christmas, as you charged for overprinting which is not referred to for the goods I ordered.' (See key technique 2.)

The matter was passed to a director.

'We are sorry to hear you are unhappy with the company. Our offer sheet was rushed out and we overlooked the requirement to refer to our terms. You are correct in identifying a discrepancy in our catalogue. Unfortunately this was not noticed until after the printing had been completed, but we felt our customers would appreciate that even though it does not state this, the additional charge would apply.' (See key technique 3.)

Key techniques

1. Treating a genuine customer query in this dismissive way, as well as ignoring one of the points raised, merely stores up trouble for the future with some customers. It may solve the problem with others but it is a high-risk tactic since those that it does not satisfy will be even more annoyed.

2. The irritation caused by the dismissive approach is the direct cause of the customer investigating further. The company must either try to justify the three matters, or to negotiate (rather than impose) a way out of it.

3. It is foolish to admit to one mistake as a basis for arguing regarding another, let alone to make the assumption that 'customers would assume the terms'. The whole negotiation would have been far better and more swiftly resolved with an apology.

Case study: Know your terms!

Having advertised regularly in a magazine for some years, the agency was advised that the owners of the magazine had changed. Subsequently, during the UK recession, the agency decided to suspend advertising for two issues and received the following reply:

'We note that you wish to suspend your advertising. Since you are cancelling your advertisement, I must advise you that there will be a cancellation charge and you will be required to repay your series discount.'

'But we have never agreed any terms with your company.'

'Yes you have. The terms state that late cancellation leads to a 25% charge and cancellation of a series leads to repayment of the series discount.'

'I am sorry but I must disagree. You are referring, incorrectly, to the terms issued by your predecessors. No terms have been issued by your company.'

'For the pittance of commission I am paid, I am not going to provide new terms for the one instance where an absence of goodwill leads to this kind of problem.'

'That is completely irrelevant. Normally this would be a question of contractual commitments, but in this case there is no formal contract. However, leaving this aside, even if we accept your predecessor's terms, they do not set out the charges that you have indicated. Only if there is late cancellation is there a charge, and although one understandably loses the series discount, those terms do not indicate that the customer must repay the discount obtained earlier.'

'You have cancelled late.'

'I am sorry, but I cannot accept that. We told you of our decision more than six weeks before publication date.'

'We need to know six weeks before copy date.'

'But that is not what your predecessor's terms state. They refer to six weeks before 'publication date'. I gave you notice over three months before one publication date and over six months before the other.'

'Well, we rely on the goodwill of our customers and I don't accept this kind of close analysis of terms.'

'But the terms govern the contract, and besides it was your analysis of those terms that led to this discussion. That analysis was totally incorrect – hence our querying it. I repeat that we gave several months' notice of suspension of our advert, having advertised every quarter in your magazine for several years. As a customer of some long standing I feel we are entitled to better consideration than that evidenced by this conversation.'

Key technique

Those who seek to argue on the basis of the content of their terms need to know those terms. If you don't know the terms before you start negotiating regarding them, then almost certainly you will lose the contest.

On the other hand...

Easily understandable, jargon-free and fair terms are not only a benefit to the customer, they are also of decided benefit to those who may have to argue the organisation's case should there be queries. Whether user-friendly or not, however, before negotiating regarding disputes, it is essential that the negotiator is completely conversant with the terms. It is also important to remember that it is a lot less expensive to find a repeat sale than to generate a new sale. If there is a dispute over terms, not only is that a problem regarding the existing contract, it may impair a continuation of the relationship and future orders – the supply of customers is rarely infinite.

Testing the water: leaks

Introduction

Both in and out of negotiation encounters human beings tend to be susceptible to conditioning, or our reactions can be manipulated by the perceptive. During negotiations, actions lead to reactions that tend to cause further reactions. Thus our own reactions may to a large extent depend on the reaction of the other party. If that person does not react in the way we expect our own game plan in moving towards our desired result may be impaired. Thus if we can find out a likely reaction before we enter the negotiating encounter we will have information that we can use to plan our further moves.

Knowing without knowing

The principle of the leak is well-known in government circles and consists of a device whereby information that is supposed to be confidential is made available either to a few confidantes or a wider circle with the deliberate intention of generating a reaction. In such instances the leaked information tends to find its way into the media and thus not only can the reaction of those invited to comment be assimilated but so also can public opinion be harnessed.

Following consideration of the reaction, an official 'line' can be devised. If there is a general and vociferous outcry in total opposition to the item then the 'originator' (because they are only indirectly linked to the news) has the flexibility to:

(a) deny that the information contained in the leak was ever official policy (in such circumstances it was only a 'discussion document' that was leaked)

(b) ignore the leaked information and make proposals which may well be a watered-down version of the original facts.

Ignore rumour – pay attention to it!

It is even possible for the perpetrator to add advice that 'no notice should be taken of rumours' well knowing that such advice is similar in terms of pointlessness to the judges admonition to the jurors 'Members of the jury, please disregard that statement'. The one thing people will not do is ignore rumour (or disregard statements) and telling them that they should do either may well have the opposite effect to that intended. In the case of the deliberate leak the advice to ignore rumour is itself meant to be ignored.

Example

As this book was being drafted the media were made aware that the independent pay body responsible for setting Members of Parliament's salaries was about to recommend substantial increases. Whether the announcement was deliberate or not the effect was that for 24 hours before the matter was due to be commented upon in the House of Commons, public comment was available to help determine the 'official' line on the pay increases being suggested.

Involuntary leaks

In planning negotiations it may be necessary to discuss tactics, request information and obtain data to supplement one's own knowledge. It cannot be assumed that those involved in this information search will not in turn either deliberately or accidentally relay the information – or simply the request for it, which provides a message of its own – to the other side. For example in employer–employee negotiations, a request to the Personnel Department to provide details of absenteeism over the last year immediately conveys one or more of a number of messages:

(a) that there is about to be a clamp down on absenteeism

(b) that there may be redundancies, absenteeism being one of a number of criteria often used to determine choice of those to go

(c) that there will be strong resistance to the next wage increase request on grounds of poor attendance.

If this information is conveyed to the employees' representatives they will have an opportunity to prepare their own case and comments before the actual negotiations. In such an instance the originator needs either to ensure confidentiality or, since it might be that it is perceived to be advantageous that the other side do know of the request, deliberately not to state that the request is confidential (although one cannot assume that there will be a leak in such circumstances.

Case study: Don't assume

A company had been taken over and a director was working out his notice with the predator winding up various activities. One of these included the sale of part of his old company to a third party whom he knew quite well. At no time did the predator state that anything they said was confidential and openly discussed their selling tactics with him. Having greater regard for the third party than the predator, the director fed through to the third party the tactics that were going to be used.

Of course one will never know if the leak was accidental in that the predator assumed a confidentiality that was not present, or gambled on the fact that the matters would be fed back and 'leaked' deliberately.

Thinking time (or 'take five')

Introduction

The essential feature of modern jazz pianist Dave Brubeck's famous hit 'Take Five' was the five beats to the bar rhythm that is fairly unusual. The words have more recently come to suggest leaving a matter for a few minutes whilst a rest or review is taken. This is far less unusual and perhaps within negotiations it would be wise to use the device even more regularly. Whilst many are able to think fairly quickly, few of us can appreciate all the implications of a course of action or development within a negotiation – particularly when we are responding to a suggestion rather than initiating it.

Reaction problems

In most negotiation encounters there tends to be an initiator and a reactor. There is no doubt that the initial advantage lies with the person making a suggestion – the initiator – since they have as much time as they need to think of all aspects of the matter, to invent responses to the likely questions and determine defences to counter-attacks and contentions and so on.

If we are the respondent, however, we are in a far less advantageous situation. Unless we can anticipate what we may need to face in such a negotiation encounter we need to think very quickly and to try to see all aspects of what is occurring. This is not always possible and trying to determine all the snags whilst someone is continuing to talk and possibly put other matters to us can be extremely difficult.

Almost certainly we will need time to think about what has been suggested and to consider all the various alternatives. However, the fact that we are in face-to-face negotiation tends to create a 'pressure to conclude' which may not be in our best interests – this is when we should 'take five' and think it through.

Case study: Property legerdemain

A manager was endeavouring to divest a company of a number of properties at a time when there was a slump in the property market. In one deal he had been able to parcel three units – one very good, one average and one poor – as a composite deal.

The purchaser subsequently requested that different values be assigned to the three units than those originally quoted for the sale. The manager agreed to this on the basis that the deal would proceed within 14 rather than 21 days (see CONCESSIONS) and this was accepted.

Pressing on with the attempted sales of other units, the manager was disturbed in the middle of the construction of a very complicated 15-unit deal by the purchaser of the first deal confirming that they wanted to exchange contracts virtually immediately but would prefer to separate the three deals. Without thinking the matter through, his mind still on the advantage of speed of completion and indeed of difficult aspects of the other and larger deal, the manager agreed and the sale of the best and second-best units proceeded within the time stipulated. However, having completed on the two sales, the purchaser withdrew from the third – the poor unit – and the manager realised to his horror that in allowing a composite deal to be split into three separate deals and allowing the purchaser to reassign values, lower values had been put on the better units and a higher value on the poor unit.

Effectively the two better units had been sold at a discount leaving the company with the poorest unit.

Key technique:

Had the manager 'taken five' to think through the implications of the double change, which had been concealed to some extent by the purchaser's willingness to move quickly, the ploy might have been spotted. He was also less than happy with his professional advisers who hadn't spotted the device either.

Checklist of devices for gaining time

1. 'I'll have to call you back.' This is a bit lame and it might be better to use (2) below.

2. 'I will call you back in the next few minutes.' (This indicates a definite decision – and also an end to the present conversation).

3. 'This is an interesting point and I must give it some quiet thought – I'll come back to you shortly.'

4. 'I'll need to refer that point to higher authority for a decision.'

5. 'Sorry, I was distracted myself – someone just asked me for some information – could you just run through that for me again.'

6. 'Now that's a very interesting...' (but at this point you cut the connection as if disconnected whilst you were speaking.) If you leave your phone off the hook this should give some time for thought. However, the device can really only be used once on each caller and it would be as well to ring the caller back as soon as possible and as soon as you have thought!

7. Catch your breath and start coughing and gasp out that you need to get a drink of water and will come straight back.

8. 'Terribly sorry, I have only just popped out of a meeting to get some papers. I can't talk now I'll get back in to you [state time – and make sure the promise is fulfilled]. If the time is near the half hour or hour it might be believable to state that you are just about to go into a meeting but at other times this is less believable – especially if it is nearly lunch-time.

9. 'Sorry, I've just started an interview. I can't break off now. I'll ring you back as soon as I am free.'

10. 'Sorry, I'm in the middle of a rush job for the chairman and I really cannot stop now – I will ring you back...'

11. Arrange a code with your secretary so that (s)he can break into the conversation with an 'urgent request' for you to go somewhere or see someone.

12. 'Sorry, the chairman has just walked into the office – I'll get back to you.'